■ SCHOLASTIC

Writing to Prompts in the Trait-Based Classroom Literature Response

**Prompts That Provide All the Elements
Students Need to Start Writing:
A *Role, Audience, Format, Topic*, and *Strong Verb* (R.A.F.T.S.)**

by Ruth Culham & Amanda Wheeler

NEW YORK • TORONTO • LONDON • AUCKLAND • SYDNEY
MEXICO CITY • NEW DELHI • HONG KONG • BUENOS AIRES

Teaching *Resources*

DEDICATION

To my friends with great gobs of love and appreciation —rc

*To dedicated teachers everywhere who inspire and
encourage students each and every day —aw*

ACKNOWLEDGMENT

As teachers across the country participate in the National Writing Projects, they share
ideas for teaching students about writing. The seed for this book was planted through the
Montana Writing Project and the early, groundbreaking work of Nancy Vendeventer, a
former teacher in Bozeman, Montana, in 1979. This text is an extension of that work and
a reflection of how extensively this strategy for inspiring writers and writing has been
integrated into the everyday life of teachers and students.

Cover design by Maria Lilja
Interior design by Holly Grundon
Interior photo by Tom Hurst via SODA

ISBN 0-439-55683-x
Copyright © 2003 by The Writing Traits Company
All rights reserved. Published by Scholastic Inc.
Printed in the U.S.A.

2 3 4 5 6 7 8 9 10   40   09 08 07 06 05 04

Contents

Contents

Introduction

Getting students to write and keeping them writing is a challenge. Typically, they need help learning how to narrow their topics so they are manageable, how to organize their ideas so they fit their purpose for the writing, and how to use specific language that brings their ideas to life. R.A.F.T.S. can help. They help students start writing with focus, clarity, and energy.

What Are R.A.F.T.S. Prompts?

R.A.F.T.S., a classroom-tested technique for creating focused writing prompts, was first shared by Nancy Vendeventer, a talented teacher from Bozeman, Montana. Each prompt provides students with the baseline information they need to focus their writing:

- a **R**ole from which to write

- an **A**udience to address

- a **F**ormat in which to write

- a **T**opic about which to write

- a **S**trong verb that suggests the purpose of the writing

Structured but not rigid, this format gives students plenty of mental elbow room to write interesting, original pieces.

In this book, you will find 45 ready-to-use R.A.F.T.S. based on high-quality, best-loved fictional books, plus many ideas for creating your own R.A.F.T.S. We chose a mixture of traditional and contemporary titles that appeal to both boys and girls and have won many awards, including the Newbery Award and Honor. The titles are categorized by realistic fiction, historical fiction, and fantasy fiction, making it easy to integrate the ready-to-use R.A.F.T.S. into genre studies in your classroom.

How Are R.A.F.T.S. Prompts Constructed?

Constructing a R.A.F.T.S. prompt is simple:

- ◆ First, identify each component of the prompt. For example, for *Charlotte's Web* by E. B. White, you might choose these components:

Role:	Templeton
Audience:	the maintenance workers at the fair
Format:	speech
Topic:	why you deserve all of the leftover food from a day at the fair
Strong Verb:	convince

- ◆ Next, write the prompt in paragraph form. Since establishing a role for the writer is the first step, most R.A.F.T.S. prompts start with "You are . . .":

> You are Templeton the rat and have stowed away in Wilbur's
>
> crate which is going to the fair. Create a speech to convince the
>
> maintenance workers to give you all of the leftover food from a day
>
> at the fair.

- ◆ Then, underline and label the key components of the prompt to ensure that students have all of the necessary pieces to make their writing work:

> You are <u>Templeton</u> the rat and have stowed away in Wilbur's crate
>   **(Role)**
> which is going to the fair. Create a <u>speech</u> to <u>convince</u> the
>   **(Format)**   **(Strong verb)**
> <u>maintenance workers</u> to <u>give you all of the leftover food from a day</u>
>   **(Audience)**   **(Topic)**
> <u>at the fair</u>.

◆ Last, introduce the R.A.F.T.S. prompt to students by discussing the purpose of each component, and then provide enough time for them to create successful pieces. (For more information on introducing R.A.F.T.S., see pages 8–10 and 14–17.)

(For more information on introducing R.A.F.T.S., see pages 8–10 and 14–17.)

Ladies and Gentlemen of the Fair Maintenance Team:

> *Instead of throwing all that leftover food away, I have a great idea to save you time and work lifting those heavy trash cans! Just leave the lids open and we, the rats, will gobble up all the leavings. As a bonus, we will clean up any dishes or eating utensils that have been thrown away by mistake and stack them up neat and clean.*
> *Think of it: You're doing a good deed for us rats and you are getting clean dishes that would have been thrown away! It's a good deal all around.*
> *Thank you everyone!*

Templeton

A fifth grader's writing based on the *Charlotte's Web* R.A.F.T.S. prompt

R.A.F.T.S. prompts give students just the right amount of structure along with freedom to be creative—a great combination for writing success! This book places ready-to-use, literature-based prompts at your fingertips and provides quick, easy guidelines for creating and using your own prompts.

What Are the Benefits of Using R.A.F.T.S. Prompts?

There are many benefits to using R.A.F.T.S. Here, we focus on three: Helping students understand and apply the writing traits, helping them become proficient in the writing modes, and helping them connect to high-quality literature.

R.A.F.T.S. Prompts Help Students Understand and Apply the Writing Traits

R.A.F.T.S. prompts go hand-in-hand with the traits of writing. In the mid-1980s, a group of teachers from districts across the country realized it needed a reliable and accurate tool to measure student writing performance. By reading and sorting stacks of student writing into "good," "fair," and "poor" categories and then analyzing that writing closely, they identified characteristics that were common to all the pieces. What resulted from their efforts ultimately became an analytic assessment model that identifies seven key characteristics, or traits, of writing:

- **Ideas:** the meaning and development of the message

- **Organization:** the internal structure of the piece

- **Voice:** the way the writer brings the topic to life

- **Word Choice:** the specific vocabulary the writer uses to convey meaning

- **Sentence Fluency:** the way the words and phrases flow throughout the text

- **Conventions:** the mechanical correctness of the piece

- **Presentation:** the overall appearance of the work

When writing to a R.A.F.T.S. prompt, students focus on traits. Specifically:

- **Role** and **Audience** help students decide on the **voice** and **word choice**.

- **Format** helps students with the **organization** of the writing.

- **Topic** helps students zero in on the **ideas** of the writing.

- **Strong Verbs** direct students to the writing purpose (e.g. "persuade," "analyze," "predict," and "compare") and, from there, help them to write clearly using all the traits: **ideas, organization, voice, word choice, sentence fluency, conventions,** and **presentation.**

Using the language of the traits as the foundation, R.A.F.T.S. becomes a tool for you to help students generate interesting, original, and finely crafted writing.

What You Should Know and What You Might Tell Students About R.A.F.T.S.

Once you have chosen a R.A.F.T.S. prompt, introduce it to students. Start by defining each component and sharing how it links to the traits of writing. The chart on the next two pages contains ideas and language to help you get started. Once students understand how the R.A.F.T.S. components can help them focus their writing, use the prompts in this book and watch your students' writing soar!

ROLE

The Role of the writer is as varied as your imagination. Roles can be gleaned from subject-area topics, school situations, book characters, and real people—the sky's the limit. When the student assumes a role other than him- or herself, he or she must decide on the appropriate voice for the piece. When introducing the Role, remind students that the Role asks them to think about **Who is the author of this piece?**

Think about the way this author would write about the topic. What voice is just right for this piece of writing? Exuberant? Edgy? Confident? Hilarious? Serious? Considerate? The words and phrases in your writing should enhance the voice you choose. Ask yourself, "How would this person use words to express him- or herself clearly and make his or her voice heard?"

AUDIENCE

You, the teacher, are your students' typical Audience. By assigning a specific Audience, you can empower students to communicate their ideas to someone other than yourself. Encourage them to think about how best to reach their audience through voice and word choice, making sure to consider what they know about the topic. When introducing Audience to students, have them place themselves in the assigned Role, then answer the question, **Who is the audience for this writing?**

When writing to a certain Audience, keep in mind that you will need to determine the perfect match of voice and word choice to communicate your ideas. Consider the relationship between the role and the audience and the kind of voice that is most appropriate. Think about the words you will use. Should you be formal? Informal? What vocabulary should be explained? Be sure to think about not only *what* needs to be said, but also *how* it needs to be said to address a particular Audience.

FORMAT

Assigning a specific Format gives you the opportunity to help students learn about many possible organizational structures for their writing. (See "Formats to Consider When Creating Your Own Prompts," page 78.) Teach them to write brochures, directions, advertisements, letters, and so forth. By learning different Formats, students will practice organizing their ideas in many different ways. When introducing Format to students, have them think about the question **How do the ideas need to be organized?**

There are many different formats for writing. By focusing on Format, you will be practicing and learning organizational structures for your writing. Once you know the format for the piece you are going to write, ask yourself, "How do I organize this piece to achieve this particular Format? Where should it start? What goes in the middle? How will it end? What should my writing look like? What are the most important organizational issues when I write in this format?"

TOPIC

The Topic helps students focus on the details of their writing so that their idea develops as clearly as possible. The Topic should be well defined and contain clear guidelines such as: "Write a persuasive letter to the city planner and include several strong arguments for a new public swimming pool in your area." Giving students these clear guidelines helps them determine how much information they should include in order to develop their idea fully. When introducing the Topic to students, have them think about the question, **What is the main idea of the writing?**

If the Topic of your writing is to explain or inform the reader of something, ask yourself, "Have I included enough information so that the reader thinks I'm an expert?" "Do all my ideas add up to something important?" "Have I told the reader something he or she doesn't already know?" If the topic is to develop a narrative, ask yourself, "Is my story fully developed and complete?" "Have I written a story that is interesting and will hold the reader's attention?" "Have I put in just the right amount of detail?"

STRONG VERB

A Strong Verb, such as *persuade, analyze, create, predict,* or *compare,* helps students see the purpose of the writing and, from there, determine the appropriate ideas, organization, voice, word choice, sentence fluency, and conventions for their writing. (See "Strong Verbs to Consider When Creating Your Own Prompts," page 79.) Help students see how being clear about the overall purpose for the writing works hand-in-hand with each trait. By establishing a clear purpose at the beginning, students will be able to focus on the goal: creating a strong piece of writing. When introducing the Strong Verb to students, have them think about the question, **What is the purpose of the writing?**

The Strong Verb directs you to the purpose of your writing which, in turn, helps you determine the appropriate ideas, organization, voice, word choice, sentence fluency, and conventions for your writing. If, for example, the Strong Verb lets you know that your purpose is to persuade, then your writing should contain thoughtful arguments that will convince your reader of your point. Ask yourself, "What purpose for writing does the strong verb convey?" "What words can I use to help make my purpose clear?" "What voice will best suit my purpose?" "How can I construct my sentences to help bring my idea to life?" "What is the best organization to make this piece of writing really work well?" Are there things I could do with conventions to make sure that this piece of writing fulfills its purpose?"

Writing to Prompts in the Trait-Based Classroom: Literature Response Scholastic Teaching Resources

R.A.F.T.S. PROMPTS HELP STUDENTS BECOME PROFICIENT IN THE WRITING MODES

It takes lots of practice for students to become proficient in the various modes of writing: narrative, expository, persuasive, descriptive, and imaginative. You can provide practice by adding a writing mode to your prompts to help students understand whether they need to tell a story, to inform or explain, to construct an argument, to paint a picture with words, or to create a new way of seeing things. It's easy. All you need to do is add a writing mode to the Format, as we've done here for the book *Frindle* by Andrew Clements:

NARRATIVE

Role: Nick's frindle

Audience: frindles at the Penny Pantry store

Format: **narrative** short story

Topic: the day you got a new name

Strong Verb: describe

You are <u>Nick's frindle</u>. Write a <u>narrative short story</u> for the <u>frindles at the Penny Pantry store</u>
       (Role)   **(Format)**   **(Audience)**
<u>describing</u> <u>the day you got a new name</u>. Include several anecdotes to bring your story to life.
(Strong verb)   **(Topic)**

EXPOSITORY

Role: Nick

Audience: students

Format: **expository** newsletter article

Topic: the word *frindle* is going to be added to the dictionary

Strong Verb: notify

You are <u>Nick</u> and you have just been told by Webster's that <u>the word *frindle* is going to be</u>
      (Role)   **(Topic)**
<u>added to the dictionary</u>. Write an <u>expository newsletter article</u> to <u>notify</u> all of the <u>students</u> of
                                    (Format)   **(Strong verb)**   **(Audience)**
this historic event.

PERSUASIVE

Role: Mrs. Chatham (the principal)

Audience: other principals

Format: **persuasive** memo

Topic: use the word *frindle* instead of the word pen

Strong Verb: convince

You are <u>Mrs. Chatham</u>. Write a <u>persuasive memo</u> to <u>convince</u> the <u>other principals</u> in your
          (Role)   **(Format)**   **(Strong verb)**   **(Audience)**
school district to <u>use the word *frindle* to replace the word *pen*</u>.
                                                         (Topic)

DESCRIPTIVE

Role: Nick's college roommate

Audience: Mrs. Granger

Format: **descriptive** letter

Topic: Nick's face when he hears the news that the word *frindle* is in the
                   dictionary

Strong Verb: visualize

You are <u>Nick's college roommate</u>. Write a <u>descriptive letter</u> to <u>Mrs. Granger</u> to help
          (Role)   **(Format)**   **(Audience)**
her <u>visualize</u> <u>Nick's face when he hears the news that *frindle* is in the dictionary</u>.
   (Strong verb)   **(Topic)**

IMAGINATIVE

Role: Mrs. Granger

Audience: yourself

Format: **imaginative** journal entry

Topic: all the problems you anticipate having at school on the first day the
                   word *frindle* is used to replace *pen*

Strong Verb: consider

You are <u>Mrs. Granger</u>. Write an <u>imaginative journal entry</u> for <u>yourself</u> <u>considering</u> <u>all the</u>
   (Role)   **(Format)**   **(Audience)** **(Strong verb)**
<u>problems you anticipate having at school on the first day the word *frindle* is used to replace</u>
                                                      (Topic)
<u>the word *pen*</u>.

Adapting the ready-to-use R.A.F.T.S. or your own R.A.F.T.S. to support writing in the modes
is just that simple!

R.A.F.T.S. PROMPTS HELP STUDENTS CONNECT TO HIGH-QUALITY LITERATURE

When students write to R.A.F.T.S., they get a good look at how quality literature works by
exploring its parts from the inside out. For example, as they take on various roles and write
for various audiences, they learn to imagine the world through the eyes of characters and
solve problems along with them. As they write about topics that naturally evolve from the
stories, they consider the text's plot and key moments. In short, R.A.F.T.S. allow students to
explore literature in new ways by encouraging them to think about the most important
aspects of writing, as all good writers do.

R.A.F.T.S. create opportunities for students to interact meaningfully with literature.
When students read these delicious books and then write to R.A.F.T.S. based on them, they
think past what happened and who did it. They think about why things happened, what
circumstances were in place for the events to unfold as they did, and what might have to
change for things to turn out differently. Indeed, students develop high-level evaluation skills
as they reinterpret the content of these books for different audiences and different purposes.
To create an effective piece of writing, they must know the characters and story line well—
well enough to convince their intended readers of the meaning of the message. R.A.F.T.S.
provides a structure for helping students delve deeper into texts.

R.A.F.T.S. also create a place for reading and writing to intersect. The books on which
the ready-to-use prompts are based are special because they motivate students to think about
books as both tools for reading development and for modeling craft. As they read the books
and then write about the content and characters, they often fall in love with those books.
They return to favorite authors again and again. Opportunities to fall in love with words and
ideas in books is the perfect prescription for reluctant readers. Students who haven't enjoyed
reading in the past often change their tune when they're introduced to R.A.F.T.S. because the
prompts allow them to explore literature from a variety of directions—not just one assigned
by the teacher. And students who have always liked to read find that writing about their
favorite characters and stories brings them to new levels of understanding and enjoyment. It's
a win-win situation.

Ready-to-Use R.A.F.T.S. Prompts

The R.A.F.T.S. prompts on the following pages are based on contemporary books and perennial favorites read and enjoyed in classrooms across the country. Each page provides a short summary of the book, a filled-in R.A.F.T.S. grid, a R.A.F.T.S. prompt in paragraph form, a reference to a reproducible version of the prompt to photocopy and distribute to students, and optional components for creating your own prompts.

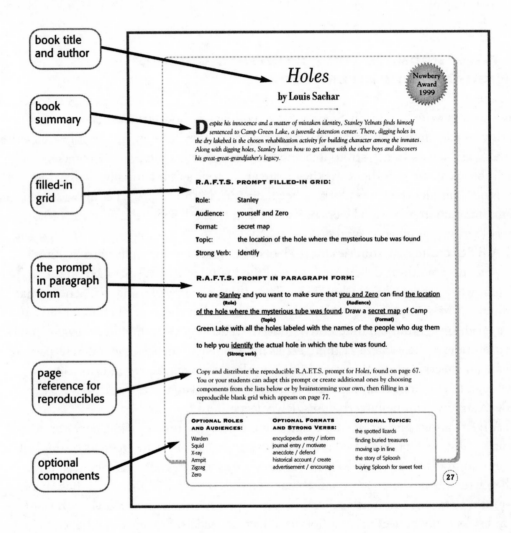

After students have read the book, write the R.A.F.T.S. prompt on the board or overhead projector, or make copies of the reproducible version (pages 66–74) and give one to each student. Review the prompt with students, encourage them to think about each component carefully, and have them organize their ideas using the Thinking Sheet on pages 16–17. From there, have them draft, revise, edit, and publish their pieces.

You can adapt these R.A.F.T.S. prompts or create new ones by choosing optional components from the lists at the bottom of each page or by brainstorming your own components. Just make copies of the blank R.A.F.T.S. grid on page 77 and fill them in.

PREWRITING THINKING FOR R.A.F.T.S. PROMPTS

Once you've introduced students to the basic idea behind R.A.F.T.S. and given them a prompt, it's time to get them thinking about what they will write. You can do this by introducing the following questions, which will help them make connections between the R.A.F.T.S. components and the information they will need to complete their writing.

(1) To understand their role in writing the piece, have students ask themselves what they know about this role. How does this person speak? What special vocabulary or language might he or she use?

(2) To understand their audience, have students ask themselves what they know about the reader for whom the piece is intended. What information does this audience need to know? What is an appropriate voice? What is the reaction students want from the audience?

(3) Have students ask themselves the best way to organize their ideas to support the format specified in the prompt. Should they present information chronologically? Should they compare and/or contrast it? Should they use deductive logic? Should they develop a central theme?

(4) To address their topic well, have students ask themselves what sorts of details to include to grab the audiences' attention. What do students already know about the topic? What questions should they answer for the reader?

(5) To understand the purpose of the piece, have students think about the strong verb. What does the strong verb suggest they do? Persuade their audience? Explain something? Describe something? Tell a story? Use their imagination?

The reproducible R.A.F.T.S. Thinking Sheet on the next two pages can help your students make these connections before they start writing. Just photocopy as many as you need.

R.A.F.T.S. Thinking Sheet

Name: _____   Date: _____   Book: _____

HOW TO USE THIS SHEET:

When you are given a R.A.F.T.S. prompt, it's important to think about each component before you start writing. For example, look at this prompt for *Charlotte's Web*:

> You are <u>Fern</u> and you want to <u>convince</u> your father that you can take care of
> **(Role)**   **(Strong verb)**
>
> a baby pig. Write a <u>list of daily chores</u> to show to your <u>father</u> that you have
>   **(Format)**   **(Audience)**
>
> thought through <u>everything you need to do to care for Wilbur</u>.
>   **(Topic)**

Then ask yourself these questions about each component:

Role: Since I'm writing as Fern, what do I know about myself and my relationship to my father?

Audience: What information does my father need to know in order to decide whether I am ready for the responsibility? What sort of voice should I use to convince him?

Format: What does a list of daily chores look like? How is it organized?

Topic: What sorts of things should be included in the list in order to convince my father that I have thought everything through?

Strong Verb: Since I am going to try to "convince" my father, my purpose is to persuade. As a writer, how do I accomplish that?

Now, by filling out this sheet, apply this thinking to the R.A.F.T.S. prompt that your teacher has given you.

(1) ROLE

What do I know about this role? _____

_____

What special language might a person in this role use? _____

_____

(2) AUDIENCE

What do I know about this audience? _____

_____

Writing to Prompts in the Trait-Based Classroom: Literature Response Scholastic Teaching Resources

What information does this audience need to know? _____

_____

What voice would be most appropriate for this audience? _____

_____

③ FORMAT

What do I know about this format? _____

_____

How are ideas typically organized for this format?

compare/contrast   cause and effect   point-by-point analysis

chronological order   deductive logic   development of a central theme

other:_____

④ TOPIC

What do I know about this topic? _____

_____

What details should I provide for my audience? _____

_____

What questions should I answer for my audience? _____

_____

Where can I go to find more information if I need it?

encyclopedias   Internet   reference materials

periodicals   an expert in the field   other:_____

newspaper   library

⑤ STRONG VERB

What purpose for my writing does this verb suggest? To inform or explain? To persuade? To describe? To tell a story? To create a new way of seeing things? Some other purpose?

_____

What key words will make my purpose clear? _____

_____

Ready-to-Use R.A.F.T.S. Prompts

Realistic Fiction

Bridge to Terabithia

by Katherine Paterson

*J*ess Aarons and Leslie Burke, once competitors in a fifth-grade running race, learn to appreciate their differences by creating a secret kingdom called Terabithia. Here they reign as king and queen, share their dreams, confront their problems, and find friendship—until tragedy strikes and they are separated forever.

R.A.F.T.S. PROMPT FILLED-IN GRID:

Role: Jess Aarons

Audience: May Belle

Format: a letter

Topic: several good reasons why she may not swing on the magic rope to Terabithia

Strong Verb: explain

R.A.F.T.S. PROMPT IN PARAGRAPH FORM:

You are <u>Jess Aarons</u> and your sister, May Belle, keeps asking to go with you to
     (Role)
Terabithia. Write <u>a letter</u> to <u>May Belle,</u> <u>explaining</u> <u>several good reasons why she</u>
     (Format)   **(Audience)** **(Strong verb)**
<u>may not swing on the magic rope to Terabithia</u> with you and Leslie.
     (Topic)

Copy and distribute the reproducible R.A.F.T.S. prompt for *Bridge to Terabithia*, found on page 66. You or your students can adapt this prompt or create additional ones by choosing components from the lists below or by brainstorming your own, then filling in a reproducible blank grid which appears on page 77.

OPTIONAL ROLES AND AUDIENCES:	OPTIONAL FORMATS AND STRONG VERBS:	OPTIONAL TOPICS:
Leslie	friendly letter / describe	Leslie's life without TV
Aaron	wanted poster / alert	the enemies of Terabithia
Janice Avery	journal entry / reflect	thoughts of moving from the city
Mrs. Myers	dialogue / divulge	to the farm
Prince Terrian	instructions / guide	losing your best friend
Judy and Bill Burke		how to get to Terabithia
Miss Edmunds		
Miss Bessie		

Dear Mr. Henshaw

by Beverly Cleary

While in the second grade, Leigh Botts wrote a letter to Boyd Henshaw, the author of Leigh's favorite book, *Ways to Amuse a Dog*. Now in the fourth grade, Leigh writes again to ask the author for some tips on writing a book as part of an assignment. This begins a correspondence with Mr. Henshaw, who tells Leigh that the way to become an author is to write. Mr. Henshaw encourages Leigh to keep a diary, in which he works out his feelings about his parents' divorce, his dad's absence, his problems at school, and his desire to become an author.

R.A.F.T.S. PROMPT FILLED-IN GRID:

Role: Leigh

Audience: best friend

Format: e-mail

Topic: feelings about your telephone conversation with your father

Strong Verb: share

R.A.F.T.S. PROMPT IN PARAGRAPH FORM:

You are <u>Leigh</u> and are very upset after talking to your dad on the telephone. Not
    (Role)
only had he not called in a while, but when he finally did, you heard a woman and

a boy in the background. Write an <u>e-mail</u> to your <u>best friend</u> <u>sharing</u> your
               (Format)   **(Audience)** **(Strong verb)**
<u>feelings about your conversation with your father</u>.
       (Topic)

Copy and distribute the reproducible R.A.F.T.S. prompt for *Dear Mr. Henshaw*, found on page 66. You or your students can adapt this prompt or create additional ones by choosing components from the lists below or by brainstorming your own, then filling in a reproducible blank grid which appears on page 77.

OPTIONAL ROLES AND AUDIENCES:	OPTIONAL FORMATS AND STRONG VERBS:	OPTIONAL TOPICS:
Leigh	diary entry / compare	the lunch bag burglar alarm
Mr. Henshaw	plan / describe	the loss of Bandit
Mr. Fridley	map / guide	being called an author by Angela Badger
Miss Neely	letter / confide	the return of Dad and Bandit
Kat	dialogue / contemplate	
Bandit		

Everything on a Waffle
by Polly Horvath

Primrose Squarp, an 11-year-old girl whose parents were lost at sea, finds herself living with an uncle who doesn't have much time for her. But things start to look up when she meets Kate, a restaurant owner who loves to serve everything on a waffle! Primrose entertains herself (and gets in trouble) by observing and commenting on the townspeople, who are not quite sure how they feel about her.

R.A.F.T.S. PROMPT FILLED-IN GRID:

Role: Primrose Squarp

Audience: restaurant patrons

Format: menu

Topic: the most appetizing of Kate's famous dishes

Strong Verb: describe

R.A.F.T.S. PROMPT IN PARAGRAPH FORM:

You are <u>Primrose Squarp</u>. Create a waffle <u>menu</u> for <u>restaurant patrons</u> <u>describing</u>
      (Role)   **(Format)**   **(Audience)**   **(Strong verb)**
<u>the most appetizing of Kate's famous dishes</u>. Don't forget to include the regular
      (Topic)
selections, dieter's selections, and children's selections on your menu.

Copy and distribute the reproducible R.A.F.T.S. prompt for *Everything on a Waffle*, found on page 66. You or your students can adapt this prompt or create additional ones by choosing components from the lists below or by brainstorming your own, then filling in a reproducible blank grid which appears on page 77.

OPTIONAL ROLES AND AUDIENCES:	OPTIONAL FORMATS AND STRONG VERBS:	OPTIONAL TOPICS:
Kate	contest entry / brainstorm	a new name for the restaurant that better suits its fare
Miss Perfidy	recipe / review	best recipe for food on a waffle
Uncle Jack	anecdote / describe	why Miss Perfidy smells like mothballs
Miss Honeycutt	journal entry / express	a typical day in Primrose's life
townspeople	dialogue / scrutinize	a conversation with the guidance counselor
restaurant patrons		
foster parents		

Fig Pudding

by Ralph Fletcher

Cliff Abernathy, the oldest of six children, narrates episodes of a bittersweet year filled with good and bad times for his family: brothers Josh, Teddy, Nate, and Brad; his sister, Cyn; his mom and dad; and Grandma Annie. The 12-year-old shares everyday family disasters, the irritations of living in a big family, and the sadness of a family member's death.

R.A.F.T.S. PROMPT FILLED-IN GRID:

Role: Teddy's brothers

Audience: Mom and Dad

Format: series of illustrations with captions

Topic: Teddy's mood and reasons for his decision to park himself under the table

Strong Verb: capture

R.A.F.T.S. PROMPT IN PARAGRAPH FORM:

<u>Teddy's brothers</u> find it amusing that he spends all of his time under the kitchen
     (Role)
table. <u>Capture</u> <u>Teddy's mood and reasons for his decision to park himself under the</u>
     (Strong verb)   (Topic)
<u>table</u> through a <u>series of illustrations with captions</u> to amuse <u>Mom and Dad</u>.
                 (Format)   (Audience)
Organize the series on a storyboard for presentation.

Copy and distribute the reproducible R.A.F.T.S. prompt for *Fig Pudding*, found on page 66. You or your students can adapt this prompt or create additional ones by choosing components from the lists below or by brainstorming your own, then filling in a reproducible blank grid which appears on page 77.

OPTIONAL ROLES AND AUDIENCES:	OPTIONAL FORMATS AND STRONG VERBS:	OPTIONAL TOPICS:
Cliff	anecdote / create	alternate meanings of "yidda yadda"
Grandma Annie	short story / contemplate	Mom making fig pudding instead of Dad
Nate	newspaper article / explain	
Brad	debate / compare	favorite things that start with *B*
Mom	letter / describe	which tastes better: Dad's fig pudding or Grandma's stollen
Josh		
Mr. Beck		all the wonderful things in Brad's Christmas stocking
Cyn		
Dad		

Frindle

by Andrew Clements

Nick Allen is an enterprising fifth grader who loves to devise time-wasting questions to avoid work in and out of class. When one of his delaying questions backfires, he's assigned an extra report that starts him on a course to introduce a new word into the English language: frindle. But Nick finds out that the process isn't so easy when his language arts teacher, Mrs. Granger, plays devil's advocate.

R.A.F.T.S. PROMPT FILLED-IN GRID:

Role: one of the students in Nick's classroom

Audience: Mrs. Granger

Format: unabridged dictionary entry

Topic: the word *frindle* and all of its possible meanings

Strong Verb: define

R.A.F.T.S. PROMPT IN PARAGRAPH FORM:

You are <u>one of the students in Nick's classroom</u>. Thanks to Nick, you have a new
                                            (Role)
word in your vocabulary. As an assignment for <u>Mrs. Granger</u>, write the complete,
                                                (Audience)
<u>unabridged dictionary entry</u>, <u>defining</u> <u>the word *frindle* and all of its possible</u>
        (Format)   **(Strong verb)**   **(Topic)**
<u>meanings</u>.

Copy and distribute the reproducible R.A.F.T.S. prompt for *Frindle*, found on page 67. You or your students can adapt this prompt or create additional ones by choosing components from the lists below or by brainstorming your own, then filling in a reproducible blank grid which appears on page 77.

OPTIONAL ROLES AND AUDIENCES:	OPTIONAL FORMATS AND STRONG VERBS:	OPTIONAL TOPICS:
Nick	advertisement / persuade	the importance of owning a frindle
fifth-grade students	short story / describe	
Mrs. Allen	commentary / summarize	the ongoing "war" between Nick and Mrs. Granger
a frindle	e-mail / convince	
Mrs. Chatham	letter / exemplify	what it's like to travel from idea to dictionary
Alice Lunderson		
Mr. Allen		getting your friends to go along with your plan
Judy Morgan		
Webster's dictionary		pride in being called a frindle

From the Mixed-up Files of
Mrs. Basil E. Frankweiler

by E. L. Konigsburg

Newbery Award 1968

Twelve-year-old Claudia Kincaid doesn't feel appreciated, so she decides to run away from home to teach her parents a lesson. But she doesn't run away to just anyplace. Claudia chooses the Metropolitan Museum of Art and, along with her brother Jamie, hides in the museum until it closes. Little do they know what mystery, adventure, and knowledge await them when they encounter a sculpture of a beautiful "angel" in the Italian Renaissance exhibit.

R.A.F.T.S. PROMPT FILLED-IN GRID:

Role: E. L. Konigsburg

Audience: your publisher

Format: memo

Topic: use the title you have selected over the three other possible titles

Strong Verb: persuade

R.A.F.T.S. PROMPT IN PARAGRAPH FORM:

You are <u>E. L. Konigsburg</u>, the author of this wonderful book. Write a <u>memo</u> that you
         (Role)   **(Format)**
will share with <u>your publisher</u> at an editorial meeting, <u>persuading</u> him to <u>use the</u>
         (Audience)   **(Strong verb)**
<u>title you have selected over the three other possible titles</u> that he likes better.
       (Topic)

Copy and distribute the reproducible R.A.F.T.S. prompt for *From the Mixed-Up Files of Mrs. Basil E. Frankweiler*, found on page 67. You or your students can adapt this prompt or create additional ones by choosing components from the lists below or by brainstorming your own, then filling in a reproducible blank grid which appears on page 77.

OPTIONAL ROLES AND AUDIENCES:	**OPTIONAL FORMATS AND STRONG VERBS:**	**OPTIONAL TOPICS:**
Jamie	brochure / excite	new sculpture at the museum
Claudia	historical account /educate	Michelangelo's sculpture of Angel
Mrs. Basil E. Frankweiler	journal entry / define	what it's like to be made of marble
Angel	instructions / inform	how to hide from museum guards
Mr. and Mrs. Kincaid	letter / apologize	
museum curator		taking coins from the fountain
Michelangelo		

Harris and Me: A Summer Remembered
by Gary Paulsen

After being dumped on his Aunt Claire and Uncle Knute's farm for the summer, an 11-year-old boy shares a first-hand account of life there. And what a summer it is—full of mischievous adventures devised by nine-year-old cousin Harris, lots of love and caring from his Aunt Clair and cousin Glennis, and hilarious encounters with the farm's animals. By the end of the summer, this outsider feels like part of the family, just when he has to leave again.

R.A.F.T.S. PROMPT FILLED-IN GRID:

Role: Harris

Audience: your cousin

Format: set of instructions

Topic: catching Ernie, the rooster, and putting him into his coop at the end of the day

Strong Verb: hoodwink

R.A.F.T.S. PROMPT IN PARAGRAPH FORM:

You are <u>Harris</u> and you think it is fun to make your citified cousin look silly. Write a
       (Role)
<u>set of instructions</u> to <u>hoodwink</u> <u>your cousin</u> into thinking that <u>Ernie, the rooster, can</u>
   (Format)   **(Strong verb)**   **(Audience)**
<u>be caught and put into his coop at the end of the day</u>. Be sure to include the reason
         (Topic)
behind each step of the instructions.

Copy and distribute the reproducible R.A.F.T.S. prompt for *Harris and Me: A Summer Remembered*, found on page 67. You or your students can adapt this prompt or create additional ones by choosing components from the lists below or by brainstorming your own, then filling in a reproducible blank grid which appears on page 77.

OPTIONAL ROLES AND AUDIENCES:	OPTIONAL FORMATS AND STRONG VERBS:	OPTIONAL TOPICS:
city cousin	anecdote / empathize	the day that Harris speared the pancakes
Claire	short story / entertain	the mystery of what happened to Harris's pants
Glennis	dialogue / compare	
Knute	journal entry / reveal	moving from the city to a farm
Minnie	contest entry / convince	
Louie		living with a family that is not your own
Vivian		

Hatchet

by Gary Paulsen

Newbery
Honor
1988

On his way to visit his father in the Canadian oil fields, a desperate 13-year-old Brian Robeson guides a small plane to a crash landing in the wilderness after the pilot suffers a heart attack. From there, Brian enters a battle for his own survival. With more brains than wilderness experience, Brian builds a shelter, makes weapons for protection, traps animals for food, and comes to terms with the simple truth that self-pity and despair can't help a person survive!

R.A.F.T.S. PROMPT FILLED-IN GRID:

Role: Brian

Audience   anyone who might ever be stranded

Format: chapter of a survival handbook

Topic: the key survival techniques you learned in the Canadian wilderness

Strong Verb: outline

R.A.F.T.S. PROMPT IN PARAGRAPH FORM:

You are <u>Brian</u> after your perilous experience. Write a <u>chapter of a survival handbook,</u>
     (Role)   **(Format)**
<u>outlining</u> <u>the key survival techniques you learned in the Canadian wilderness</u> that
(Strong verb)   **(Topic)**
<u>anyone who might ever be stranded</u> should know. Focus on food, shelter, or
                   (Audience)
protection.

Copy and distribute the reproducible R.A.F.T.S. prompt for *Hatchet*, found on page 67. You or your students can adapt this prompt or create additional ones by choosing components from the lists below or by brainstorming your own, then filling in a reproducible blank grid which appears on page 77.

OPTIONAL ROLES AND AUDIENCES:	**OPTIONAL FORMATS AND STRONG VERBS:**	**OPTIONAL TOPICS:**
Brian's mom	letter / confide	ways to make fire
Brian's dad	journal entry / review	what needs to be done each day to survive
pilot	diary entry / reflect	keeping track of all your "firsts"
bear	list / describe	what needs to be in a survival pack
hatchet	brochure / define	
Brian		

Holes

by Louis Sachar

Newbery Award 1999

*D*espite his innocence and a matter of mistaken identity, Stanley Yelnats finds himself sentenced to Camp Green Lake, a juvenile detention center. There, digging holes in the dry lakebed is the chosen rehabilitation activity for building character among the inmates. Along with digging holes, Stanley learns how to get along with the other boys and discovers his great-great-grandfather's legacy.

R.A.F.T.S. PROMPT FILLED-IN GRID:

Role:　　　　Stanley

Audience:　　yourself and Zero

Format:　　　secret map

Topic:　　　　the location of the hole where the mysterious tube was found

Strong Verb:　identify

R.A.F.T.S. PROMPT IN PARAGRAPH FORM:

You are <u>Stanley</u> and you want to make sure that <u>you and Zero</u> can find <u>the location</u>
　　　(Role)　　　　　　　　　　　　　　　(Audience)
<u>of the hole where the mysterious tube was found</u>. Draw a <u>secret map</u> of Camp
　　　　　　　　(Topic)　　　　　　　　　　　　　　　(Format)
Green Lake with all the holes labeled with the names of the people who dug them

to help you <u>identify</u> the actual hole in which the tube was found.
　　　(Strong verb)

Copy and distribute the reproducible R.A.F.T.S. prompt for *Holes*, found on page 67. You or your students can adapt this prompt or create additional ones by choosing components from the lists below or by brainstorming your own, then filling in a reproducible blank grid which appears on page 77.

OPTIONAL ROLES AND AUDIENCES:	OPTIONAL FORMATS AND STRONG VERBS:	OPTIONAL TOPICS:
Warden	encyclopedia entry / inform	the spotted lizards
Squid	journal entry / motivate	finding buried treasures
X-ray	anecdote / defend	moving up in line
Armpit	historical account / create	the story of Sploosh
Zigzag	advertisement / encourage	buying Sploosh for sweet feet
Zero		

Hoot

by Carl Hiaasen

Roy Eberhart, the new kid at Trace Middle School, encounters a series of unusual events from witnessing a running bare-footed boy to hooking up with bully-beating Beatrice to discovering burrowing owls living in the lot on the corner. Strangely connected, these events lead to an unlikely alliance to stop the construction of Mother Paula's All-American Pancake House, which is scheduled to be built over the endangered owl's burrows.

R.A.F.T.S. PROMPT FILLED-IN GRID:

Role: Roy Eberhardt and/or Beatrice Leap

Audience: people of Coconut Grove

Format: newspaper article

Topic: why Mother Paula's All-American Pancake House is moving its building site

Strong Verb: clarify

R.A.F.T.S. PROMPT IN PARAGRAPH FORM:

You are <u>Roy Eberhardt and/or Beatrice Leap</u> of Coconut Grove, Florida. In a front
        (Role)
page <u>newspaper article</u> for the <u>people of Coconut Grove,</u> <u>clarify</u> <u>why Mother Paula's</u>
   (Format)   **(Audience)**   **(Strong verb)**
<u>All-American Pancake House is moving its building site</u> from its original location to
        (Topic)
the corner of East Oriole and Woodbury.

Copy and distribute the reproducible R.A.F.T.S. prompt for *Hoot*, found on page 68. You or your students can adapt this prompt or create additional ones by choosing components from the lists below or by brainstorming your own, then filling in a reproducible blank grid which appears on page 77.

OPTIONAL ROLES AND AUDIENCES:	OPTIONAL FORMATS AND STRONG VERBS:	OPTIONAL TOPICS:
Dana Matherson	news article / inform	gators in the latrines
Curly	poster / convince	save the owls
Garrett	announcement / encourage	meeting on the Mother Paula's All-American Pancake House property
Beatrice Leep	letter / defend	
Lonna Leep	e-mail / inquire	plans to save the owls
Mullet Fingers		what happened to Mullet Fingers
students at Trace Middle School		

How to Eat Fried Worms

by Thomas Rockwell

Ten-year-old Billy Forester takes on a revolting yet intriguing bet with his friend, Joe, in order to win $50 for a minibike. He agrees to eat 15 worms in 15 days, and his friends delight in cooking up a variety of recipes that require fat, juicy worms. Appearing more confident than he is, Billy works his way to the prize—day by day and worm by worm, dousing them in ketchup, mustard, horseradish, and a dash of lemon juice.

R.A.F.T.S. PROMPT FILLED-IN GRID:

Role: Mrs. Forester

Audience: entire family

Format: speech

Topic: eating your delicious new worm recipe for dinner will help Billy get the minibike

Strong Verb: convince

R.A.F.T.S. PROMPT IN PARAGRAPH FORM:

You are <u>Mrs. Forester</u> and you realize that Billy will never win the bet for the $50.00
      (Role)
without your help. Write a <u>speech</u> to give to the <u>entire family</u>, <u>convincing</u> members
      (Format)   **(Audience)**   **(Strong verb)**
that <u>eating your delicious new worm recipe for dinner will help Billy get the mini-</u>
      (Topic)
<u>bike</u>.

Copy and distribute the reproducible R.A.F.T.S. prompt for *How to Eat Fried Worms*, found on page 68. You or your students can adapt this prompt or create additional ones by choosing components from the lists below or by brainstorming your own, then filling in a reproducible blank grid which appears on page 77.

OPTIONAL ROLES AND AUDIENCES:	**OPTIONAL FORMATS AND STRONG VERBS:**	**OPTIONAL TOPICS:**
Mr. Forester	contest entry / entice	interesting ways to cook worms
Mrs. Forester	slogan / inspire	why a worm a day is good for you
Joe	skit / amuse	
Alan	e-mail/ enlighten	the main purpose of flapping like a bird
Tom	commentary / state	
Dr. McGrath		what it's like to eat a worm
the worms		earning a minibike the hard way

Maniac Magee

by Jerry Spinelli

Newbery
Award
1991

*J*effrey Lionel "Maniac" Magee is orphaned and living with his bickering Aunt Dot and Uncle Dan. After eight long years of listening to them fight, he runs away to the small town of Two Mills, Pennsylvania. There he finds himself a folk hero of sorts after hitting a home run thrown by the town's best pitcher, untangling the famous "Cobbles Knot," and teaching old Mr. Grayson to read. But Maniac learns that there is more to Two Mills than just fun when he encounters the hatred and racism between the "Blacks" of East End and the "Whites" of West End.

R.A.F.T.S. PROMPT FILLED-IN GRID:

Role: Maniac Magee

Audience: Grayson

Format: first page of the story

Topic: *The Man Who Struck Out Willie Mays*

Strong Verb: write

R.A.F.T.S. PROMPT IN PARAGRAPH FORM:

You are <u>Maniac Magee</u>. For a Christmas present, you give <u>Grayson</u> a short story you
    (Role)   **(Audience)**
wrote about his baseball playing years, titled <u>*The Man Who Struck Out Willie Mays*</u>.
                                                 (Topic)
<u>Write</u> the <u>first page of the story</u>. To hook the reader, include the most interesting
(Strong verb)   **(Format)**
things you know about Grayson.

Copy and distribute the reproducible R.A.F.T.S. prompt for *Maniac Magee*, found on page 68. You or your students can adapt this prompt or create additional ones by choosing components from the lists below or by brainstorming your own, then filling in a reproducible blank grid which appears on page 77.

OPTIONAL ROLES AND AUDIENCES:	**OPTIONAL FORMATS AND STRONG VERBS:**	**OPTIONAL TOPICS:**
Amanda Beale	news article / embellish	the frogball four-bagger
Finsterwald	diagnosis / reveal	being allergic to pizza
John McNab	poem / describe	the colors of East End
Cobras	journal entry / investigate	the day Maniac felt racism
Mars Bar	encyclopedia entry / define	Maniac's new and final home
Hester		
Lester		

Mick Harte Was Here

by Barbara Park

Thirteen-year-old Phoebe Harte narrates the story of her younger brother, Mick, who died in a bicycle accident. The grieving Phoebe remembers Mick with love, humor, and anger. Convincingly, she shares the effects of Mick's death on her family, friends, and schoolmates.

R.A.F.T.S. PROMPT FILLED-IN GRID:

Role: Mick's best friend

Audience: family and friends

Format: eulogy

Topic: all of the great things about Mick and his life

Strong Verb: remember

R.A.F.T.S. PROMPT IN PARAGRAPH FORM:

You are <u>Mick's best friend</u> and have been asked to speak at his memorial service.
        (Role)

Write the <u>eulogy</u> that you give at the service to help the grieving <u>family and friends</u>
        (Format)   **(Audience)**

<u>remember</u> <u>all of the great things about Mick and his life</u>.
(Strong verb)   **(Topic)**

Copy and distribute the reproducible R.A.F.T.S. prompt for *Mick Harte Was Here*, found on page 68. You or your students can adapt this prompt or create additional ones by choosing components from the lists below or by brainstorming your own, then filling in a reproducible blank grid which appears on page 77.

OPTIONAL ROLES AND AUDIENCES:
Phoebe
Mick
Pop
Mother
Zoe
Wocket
Nana
Mrs. Berryhill

OPTIONAL FORMATS AND STRONG VERBS:
letter to the editor / convince
phone conversation / confess
list / characterize
short story / embellish
diary entry / describe

OPTIONAL TOPICS:
what could have prevented Mick's accident

items from Mick's past to share at the assembly

Mick's antics to make people laugh

Mick is everywhere

Tales of a Fourth Grade Nothing

by Judy Blume

Nine-year-old Peter Hatcher shares the hilarious trials and tribulations of living in the same house with a younger brother, Fudge. The problem is that grown-ups think Fudge is absolutely adorable, but Peter knows better. Fudge is actually mischief in motion. Whether he's throwing temper tantrums or eating flowers, he causes havoc everywhere he goes. Despite all of this, Fudge always seems to come out on top, leaving Peter feeling less than appreciated.

R.A.F.T.S. PROMPT FILLED-IN GRID:

Role: Peter

Audience: your parents

Format: script for a skit

Topic: some of the silly things that your brother, Fudge, does

Strong Verb: characterize

R.A.F.T.S. PROMPT IN PARAGRAPH FORM:

You are <u>Peter</u> and you want to amuse <u>your parents</u> with <u>some of the silly things your</u>
      (Role)   **(Audience)**

<u>brother, Fudge, does</u>. In a <u>script for a skit</u> that you will perform, <u>characterize</u> some of
   (Topic)   **(Format)**   **(Strong verb)**
Fudge's more zany antics.

Copy and distribute the reproducible R.A.F.T.S. prompt for *Tales of a Fourth Grade Nothing*, found on page 68. You or your students can adapt this prompt or create additional ones by choosing components from the lists below or by brainstorming your own, then filling in a reproducible blank grid which appears on page 77.

OPTIONAL ROLES AND AUDIENCES:	**OPTIONAL FORMATS AND STRONG VERBS:**	**OPTIONAL TOPICS:**
Mrs. Hatcher	advertisement / convince	a new advertisement for the wonderful taste of Juicy-O
Mr. Hatcher	dialogue / persuade	Fudge will never be able to fly like a bird
Fudge	lecture / spell out	
Tootsie	announcement / relieve	Fudge should keep out of your things
Dribble	journal entry / confess	
Jimmy Fargo		Fudge's condition after swallowing Dribble
Sheila		

Tangerine
by Edward Bloor

*T*welve-year-old Paul Fisher and his family have moved from Texas to Tangerine County, Florida, where things are really different. Tangerine has lightning that strikes the same practice field every day, muck fires with smoke that burns your eyes and nose, and sinkholes that can swallow whole schools. Paul tries to fit in and live up to big brother Erik's football legacy by playing soccer even though he wears thick glasses because of an eye injury that he can't remember suffering. But Paul soon learns that Erik is not what he seems to be and begins a journey of discovery about dark family secrets and his unremembered past.

R.A.F.T.S. PROMPT FILLED-IN GRID:

Role: Paul

Audience: yourself

Format: top-ten list

Topic: skills and contributions as a soccer player, friend, family member, and citizen of the town of Tangerine

Strong Verb: examine

R.A.F.T.S. PROMPT IN PARAGRAPH FORM:

You are <u>Paul</u> and you have just been kicked off the soccer team. Write a <u>top-ten list</u>
    (Role) and (Audience)   **(Format)**
of your <u>skills and contributions as a soccer player, friend, family member, and citizen</u>
                                        (Topic)
<u>of the town of Tangerine</u>. In your list, <u>examine</u> how your poor eyesight impacts
                                        (Strong verb)
people's perceptions of you and your skills and contributions.

Copy and distribute the reproducible R.A.F.T.S. prompt for *Tangerine*, found on page 69. You or your students can adapt this prompt or create additional ones by choosing components from the lists below or by brainstorming your own, then filling in a reproducible blank grid which appears on page 77.

OPTIONAL ROLES AND AUDIENCES:	**OPTIONAL FORMATS AND STRONG VERBS:**	**OPTIONAL TOPICS:**
Mom	anecdote / construct	the origin of the eclipse story
Dad	skit / alert	the sinkhole that swallowed a school
Erik	news article / inform	
Arthur	journal entry / scrutinize	Dad turning a blind eye to Erik's problem
Joey	announcement / introduce	
Coach Warner		Paul's acceptance on the team

The Outsiders

by S. E. Hinton

Ponyboy Curtis, who is tough on the outside and sensitive on the inside, shares the daily conflicts of the East Side Greasers (outsiders) and the rich West Side Socs (socials). Fourteen-year-old Ponyboy and his brothers, Darry and Soda, are Greasers and must constantly defend themselves and their friends against harassment from the Socs. Then, all in one week, things go too far and three are dead, leaving Ponyboy to ponder the futility of gang violence and the value of family.

R.A.F.T.S. PROMPT FILLED-IN GRID:

Role: Soda

Audience   Darry and Ponyboy

Format: speech

Topic: what their fighting is doing to you and the family

Strong Verb: enlighten

R.A.F.T.S. PROMPT IN PARAGRAPH FORM:

Darry and Ponyboy have been fighting ever since their parents died and Darry stepped in as head of the family. As <u>Soda</u>, write a <u>speech</u> to <u>enlighten</u> <u>Darry and</u>
                  (Role)   **(Format)**   **(Strong verb)** **(Audience)**
<u>Ponyboy</u> about <u>what their fighting is doing to you and the family</u>. Include specific
                         (Topic)
instances of their fighting and how they made you feel.

Copy and distribute the reproducible R.A.F.T.S. prompt for *The Outsiders*, found on page 69. You or your students can adapt this prompt or create additional ones by choosing components from the lists below or by brainstorming your own, then filling in a reproducible blank grid which appears on page 77.

OPTIONAL ROLES AND AUDIENCES:	OPTIONAL FORMATS AND STRONG VERBS:	OPTIONAL TOPICS:
Ponyboy	dialogue / consider	the danger of talking to Cherry at the Nightly Double
Darry	commentary / compare	why their father named them Ponyboy and Sodapop
Two-bit	biographical sketch / entertain	
Johnny	debate / argue	why Cherry might think it is rough everywhere, and not just for greasers
Dally	journal entry / contemplate	
Cherry		
Marcia		

The View from Saturday

by E. L. Konigsburg

Four brilliant but shy sixth graders—Noah, Nadia, Ethan, and Julian—are chosen by their teacher, Mrs. Olinski, to participate in an academic contest. Each one tells his or her own story of the events that follow, resulting in multiple viewpoints of self-revelation, friendship, confidence, and success.

R.A.F.T.S. PROMPT FILLED-IN GRID:

Role: Mrs. Olinski

Audience: students, staff, and parents

Format: poster

Topic: the unique strengths and qualities of each person selected for the team

Strong Verb: introduce

R.A.F.T.S. PROMPT IN PARAGRAPH FORM:

You are <u>Mrs. Olinski</u> and want <u>students, staff, and parents</u> to learn about the
       (Role)   **(Audience)**

academic team you have chosen. <u>Introduce</u> the members of the team through a
               (Strong verb)

<u>poster</u> that highlights <u>the unique strengths and qualities of each person selected for</u>
(Format)   **(Topic)**

<u>the team</u>.

Copy and distribute the reproducible R.A.F.T.S. prompt for *The View From Saturday*, found on page 69. You or your students can adapt this prompt or create additional ones by choosing components from the lists below or by brainstorming your own, then filling in a reproducible blank grid which appears on page 77.

OPTIONAL ROLES AND AUDIENCES:

Noah
Ethan
Nadia
Julian
Mrs. Laurencin
Academic Bowl emcee
Mrs. Olinski
classmates

OPTIONAL FORMATS AND STRONG VERBS:

letter / thank
journal entry / confide
interview / inquire
newspaper article / reveal
commentary / describe

OPTIONAL TOPICS:

reasons you think you and your teammates were chosen

how Mrs. Olinski feels her accident has made her a stronger person

how the team prepared for the contest

the reactions of the team during the Academic Bowl

What Jamie Saw

by Carolyn Coman

Newbery Honor 1996

Nine-year-old Jamie awakens in the middle of the night to see his mother's boyfriend, Van, pick up his crying baby sister, Nin, and throw her through the air. Luckily, mother was there to catch her, and she immediately packs up the children and moves to a small trailer in the middle of nowhere. Each day brings new challenges to the frightened family, but a close friend, Earl, brings food and checks on them from time to time. Then one day Van shows up at the trailer . . . and everything changes.

R.A.F.T.S. PROMPT FILLED-IN GRID:

Role: Jamie

Audience: yourself

Format: diary entry

Topic: how you feel about the night Van threw your baby sister, Nin

Strong Verb: explain

R.A.F.T.S. PROMPT IN PARAGRAPH FORM:

As <u>Jamie</u>, write a <u>diary entry</u> to <u>explain</u> <u>how you feel about the night Van threw your</u>
(Role) and (Audience)   (Format)   (Strong verb)   (Topic)
<u>baby sister, Nin</u>. Be sure to include how you might tell your mom about your fears

and concerns, without upsetting her more than she already is.

Copy and distribute the reproducible R.A.F.T.S. prompt for *What Jamie Saw*, found on page 69. You or your students can adapt this prompt or create additional ones by choosing components from the lists below or by brainstorming your own, then filling in a reproducible blank grid which appears on page 77.

OPTIONAL ROLES AND AUDIENCES:	OPTIONAL FORMATS AND STRONG VERBS:	OPTIONAL TOPICS:
Jamie	advertisement / encourage	Patty, Nin, and Jamie need a place to stay
Mrs. Desrochers	telegram / alert	Jamie's need to return to school
Van	letter / express	what happened the night they left
Nin	review / defend	
Patty	telephone conversation / contemplate	what Patty would have told Agnus about Van
Earl		
Agnus		

Where the Red Fern Grows:
The Story of Two Dogs and a Boy
by Wilson Rawls

Billy Colman, a ten-year old boy growing up in the Ozark Mountains of Oklahoma, works hard for two years to scrimp and save $50 for a pair of coonhound pups. Carefree days follow as the boy and his dogs try to "tree" the local raccoons. In time, this inseparable team wins the sought-after gold cup in the annual coon-hunt contest, captures the tricky ghost coon, and comes face to face with a mountain lion. But tragedy strikes and, while Billy grieves, he finds solace in a Native American legend.

R.A.F.T.S. PROMPT FILLED-IN GRID:

Role: breeder/owner

Audience: prospective dog owners, including Grandpa

Format: advertisement

Topic: information they need about your coonhound pups

Strong Verb: advise

R.A.F.T.S. PROMPT IN PARAGRAPH FORM:

You are the <u>breeder/owner</u> of some coonhound pups. Create an <u>advertisement</u> that
          (Role)   **(Format)**
will <u>advise</u> <u>prospective dog owners, including Grandpa</u>, of all the <u>information they</u>
  (Strong verb)   **(Audience)**   **(Topic)**
<u>need about your coonhound pups</u>. Be sure to include some good reasons to buy

your pups instead of other breeders'.

Copy and distribute the reproducible R.A.F.T.S. prompt for *Where the Red Fern Grows: The Story of Two Dogs and a Boy*, found on page 69. You or your students can adapt this prompt or create additional ones by choosing components from the lists below or by brainstorming your own, then filling in a reproducible blank grid which appears on page 77.

OPTIONAL ROLES AND AUDIENCES:	OPTIONAL FORMATS AND STRONG VERBS:	OPTIONAL TOPICS:
Billy	journal entry / boast	whether your dogs are suited for the annual contest
Grandpa	debate / defend	hunting the ghost coon
Mama	directions / divulge	facing the mountain lion
Papa	newspaper article / summarize	why the red fern picked the graves of Little Ann and Old Dan to grow on
Old Dan	poem / reflect	
Little Ann		
Rubin Pritchard		

Ready-to-Use
R.A.F.T.S. Prompts

Historical

Fiction

A Year Down Yonder

by Richard Peck

Newbery Award 2001

It's 1937 and 15-year-old Mary Alice is sent to stay in rural Illinois with her feisty and sometimes outrageous Grandma Dowdel, while her brother Joey goes off to work in the Civilian Conservation Corps. During her visit, Mary Alice evolves from a cautious "rich kid from Chicago" into a willing accomplice in her grandma's madcap schemes to do good while no one is looking.

R.A.F.T.S. PROMPT FILLED-IN GRID:

Role: Grandma Dowdel

Audience: Mary Alice

Format: summary

Topic: your new, wacky scheme to help the town

Strong Verb: convince

R.A.F.T.S. PROMPT IN PARAGRAPH FORM:

You are <u>Grandma Dowdel</u> and you want Mary Alice to buy into <u>your new, wacky</u>
                 (Role)
<u>scheme to help the town</u>. Write a <u>summary</u> of your scheme to <u>convince</u> Mary Alice
        (Topic)   **(Format)**   **(Strong verb) (Audience)**
that it's a good idea and that everything will turn out alright.

Copy and distribute the reproducible R.A.F.T.S. prompt for *A Year Down Yonder*, found on page 70. You or your students can adapt this prompt or create additional ones by choosing components from the lists below or by brainstorming your own, then filling in a reproducible blank grid which appears on page 77.

OPTIONAL ROLES AND AUDIENCES:	OPTIONAL FORMATS AND STRONG VERBS:	OPTIONAL TOPICS:
Grandma Dowdel	letter / concern	sleeping in the attic
Mary Alice	diary entry / relate	moving from Chicago
Joey	editorial / entertain	Grandma's antics
townspeople	newspaper article / analyze	hick-town school problems
classmates	short story / adapt	friends and enemies
principal		
Bootsie		

Across Five Aprils

by Irene Hunt

N ine-year-old Jethro Creighton and his family are living on an Illinois farm at the
beginning of the Civil War. As this terrible war progresses, older brothers Tom and
John and cousin Eb fight for the North, and brother Bill fights for the South. As a result, the
Creighton family faces harassment from the locals and tries to remain strong during the five
years of the Civil War.

R.A.F.T.S. PROMPT FILLED-IN GRID:

Role: Bill

Audience: the townspeople

Format: letter to the editor

Topic: your choice to fight for the South

Strong Verb: defend

R.A.F.T.S. PROMPT IN PARAGRAPH FORM:

You are <u>Bill</u> and have been told by your brother that the family is hearing a lot of
    (Role)
unfavorable talk about <u>your choice to fight for the South</u>. Write a <u>letter to the editor</u>
         (Topic)   **(Format)**
of the local paper <u>defending</u> your decision in hopes that <u>the townspeople</u> will read
    (Strong verb)   **(Audience)**
it and understand why you made this choice.

Copy and distribute the reproducible R.A.F.T.S. prompt for *Across Five Aprils*, found
on page 70. You or your students can adapt this prompt or create additional ones by
choosing components from the lists below or by brainstorming your own, then filling
in a reproducible blank grid which appears on page 77.

OPTIONAL ROLES AND AUDIENCES:	OPTIONAL FORMATS AND STRONG VERBS:	OPTIONAL TOPICS:
Ellen	diary entry / express	being allowed to eat at "first table"
Matt	newspaper article / empathize	
Jenny	telegram / assure	why Tom, John, and Eb chose to fight for the North
Tom	dialogue / inquire	
John	obituary / relate	being called Copperheads
Nancy		
Eb		the death of a president

Bud, Not Buddy

by Christopher Paul Curtis

Newbery Award 2000

Ten-year-old Bud, not Buddy, Caldwell is an orphan on the run from foster homes in Michigan in the 1930s. He has his heart set on finding his real father, whom he thinks is a bass player for a band called The Dusky Devastators of the Depression. Guided only by the band's flier, which he keeps in his worn-out suitcase, Bud hits the road to find a dad he's never met and encounters all sorts of trouble along the way.

R.A.F.T.S. PROMPT FILLED-IN GRID:

Role: Bud

Audience: TV viewers

Format: a plea

Topic: information that might lead to the discovery of the whereabouts of your dad, Herman E. Calloway

Strong Verb: appeal

R.A.F.T.S. PROMPT IN PARAGRAPH FORM:

As <u>Bud,</u> write a two-minute <u>plea</u> to be played on a local television station,
   (Role)   (Format)

<u>appealing</u> to <u>TV viewers</u> to contact you with <u>information that might lead to the</u>
(Strong verb)   (Audience)

<u>discovery of the whereabouts of your dad, Herman E. Calloway</u>.
                  (Topic)

Copy and distribute the reproducible R.A.F.T.S. prompt for *Bud, Not Buddy,* found on page 70. You or your students can adapt this prompt or create additional ones by choosing components from the lists below or by brainstorming your own, then filling in a reproducible blank grid which appears on page 77.

OPTIONAL ROLES AND AUDIENCES:	**OPTIONAL FORMATS AND STRONG VERBS:**	**OPTIONAL TOPICS:**
foster parents	editorial / describe	what it's like to be on the lam
Herman Calloway	list / clarify	life in a cardboard city
Miss Hill	anecdote / illuminate	the meaning of a special saxophone in a tattered case
Todd Amos	biographical sketch / characterize	
Mr. (Lefty) Lewis	journal entry / relate	a day in the life of Bud Caldwell
Bugs		additional rules for "Making a Funner Life and Making a Better Liar Out of Yourself"
people of Shantytown		
Mr. Jimmy		

Crispin: The Cross of Lead

Newbery Award 2003

by Avi

As wretchedly poor Crispin mourns the loss of his mother, he is befriended by Father Quinel and begins a journey that puts him in mortal danger, changes his future, and calls into question the fourteenth-century feudal system of governing. Along the way, Crispin meets a huge, red-bearded man nicknamed Bear. The two of them cross the English countryside together, seeking to rendezvous with other radicals who want to overthrow Lord Furnival's heir and create a more democratic England.

R.A.F.T.S. PROMPT FILLED-IN GRID:

Role: Father Quinel

Audience: Crispin

Format: speech

Topic: who his mother and father really were

Strong Verb: reveal

R.A.F.T.S. PROMPT IN PARAGRAPH FORM:

Although Father Quinel never got the opportunity to tell Crispin <u>who his mother and father really were</u>, he had the speech all planned. Write this <u>speech</u>, <u>revealing</u> all of
      (Topic)   (Format) (Strong verb)
Crispin's family secrets, and deliver it the way <u>Father Quinel</u> would have to <u>Crispin</u>:
                                                (Role)   (Audience)
through the window of the church confession booth.

Copy and distribute the reproducible R.A.F.T.S. prompt for *Crispin: The Cross of Lead*, found on page 70. You or your students can adapt this prompt or create additional ones by choosing components from the lists below or by brainstorming your own, then filling in a reproducible blank grid which appears on page 77.

OPTIONAL ROLES AND AUDIENCES:	**OPTIONAL FORMATS AND STRONG VERBS:**	**OPTIONAL TOPICS:**
Crispin	government documents / examine	why only the noble class was allowed to read and write
Bear	writing on the cross / describe	story of Crispin's mother and father told by the villagers as they remembered it
the Widow Daventry	folk tale / explain	
John Ball	castle map / create	
Lord Furnival's wife	decree / inform	how Bear got involved in overturning the feudal government
John Aycliffe		
villagers		
soldiers		

Homeless Bird

by Gloria Whelan

*K*oly, *a 13-year old girl from India, meets her sickly husband-to-be and his family for the first time on her wedding day. When her new husband dies, Koly finds herself living with her harsh and scolding mother-in-law, Sass, with no way to return to her family. When Sass tires of the daughter-in-law she never really wanted, she abandons her. Koly soon realizes that she must take charge of her own destiny. With perseverance, determination, and an exceptional talent for embroidery, she learns to support herself and shape her own life.*

R.A.F.T.S. PROMPT FILLED-IN GRID:

Role: Koly

Audience: prospective employer

Format: résumé

Topic: your many skills, especially in embroidery

Strong Verb: highlight

R.A.F.T.S. PROMPT IN PARAGRAPH FORM:

You are <u>Koly</u> and you realize you need to learn to support yourself now that you
    (Role)

have been abandoned by Sass. Write a <u>résumé</u> <u>highlighting</u> <u>your many skills,</u>
                (Format)   **(Strong verb)**

<u>especially in embroidery,</u> to encourage a <u>prospective employer</u> to hire you.
    (Topic)   **(Audience)**

Copy and distribute the reproducible R.A.F.T.S. prompt for *Homeless Bird*, found on page 70. You or your students can adapt this prompt or create additional ones by choosing components from the lists below or by brainstorming your own, then filling in a reproducible blank grid which appears on page 77.

OPTIONAL ROLES AND AUDIENCES:	OPTIONAL FORMATS AND STRONG VERBS:	OPTIONAL TOPICS:
Maa	diary entry / confess	having to marry someone you have never met
Baap	letter / communicate	how to cure sickness
Hari	instructions / divulge	what is expected of widows
Sassur	rules / clarify	the story of the new dowry quilt
Mr. Lal	short story / summarize	letting your parents know that you're alright
Tanu		
Raji		

Homesick: My Own Story

by Jean Fritz

*J*ean Fritz's own childhood memories spark a fictional story of a ten-year-old girl living in 1920s China. Although born in Hankow, China, where her American father was the director of the YMCA, the young narrator considers herself an American and longs to see a grandmother who lives in Pennsylvania. During her last two years in China, she shares compelling stories of her friends, her family, and her beloved nurse, while living in a country becoming less and less tolerant of foreigners.

R.A.F.T.S. PROMPT FILLED-IN GRID:

Role: Jean

Audience: Grandma

Format: letter

Topic: talking your dad into coming back to America immediately

Strong Verb: convince

R.A.F.T.S. PROMPT IN PARAGRAPH FORM:

As <u>Jean</u>, write a <u>letter</u> to <u>Grandma</u> to <u>convince</u> her that <u>talking your dad into coming</u>
   (Role)   (Format)   (Audience)   (Strong verb)   (Topic)
<u>back to America immediately</u> is a good idea. Include a couple of "narrow squeaks"

that will help drive your point home.

Copy and distribute the reproducible R.A.F.T.S. prompt for *Homesick: My Own Story*, found on page 71. You or your students can adapt this prompt or create additional ones by choosing components from the lists below or by brainstorming your own, then filling in a reproducible blank grid which appears on page 77.

OPTIONAL ROLES AND AUDIENCES:	**OPTIONAL FORMATS AND STRONG VERBS:**	**OPTIONAL TOPICS:**
Mother	free verse poem / imagine	how to survive "narrow squeaks"
Dad	survival guide / urge	worry for China and all of the things you have grown up with
Grandma	editorial / contemplate	
Lin Nai-Nai	diary entry / confess	feelings when looking back at China from the deck of the ship
Yang Sze-Fu	advertisement / excite	
Ian Forbes		the best things about moving to a brand-new country
Andrea		
Millie (Lee)		

Number the Stars

by Lois Lowry

Newbery Award 1990

In this fictional account of a true story, ten-year-old Annemarie Johansen and her best friend, Ellen Rosen, share their hopes and dreams just like any other young girls. But it's prewar Denmark and their world soon becomes a more dangerous place full of interrogations, food shortages, Nazi soldiers, and fear. A courageous Annemarie finds herself facing the biggest challenge of her young life when she is sent on a dangerous mission to help save Ellen and her Jewish family from certain death.

R.A.F.T.S. PROMPT FILLED-IN GRID:

Role: Annemarie

Audience: the Danish resistance

Format: news article

Topic: how to obtain a special handkerchief

Strong Verb: inform

R.A.F.T.S. PROMPT IN PARAGRAPH FORM:

You are <u>Annemarie</u>. Write a <u>news article</u> for *De Frie Danske* secretly <u>informing</u>
     (Role)   (Format)   (Strong verb)
<u>the Danish resistance</u> of <u>how to obtain a special handkerchief</u>. Try not to give
      (Audience)   (Topic)
away any secrets to Nazi soldiers who might read the article.

Copy and distribute the reproducible R.A.F.T.S. prompt for *Number the Stars*, found on page 71. You or your students can adapt this prompt or create additional ones by choosing components from the lists below or by brainstorming your own, then filling in a reproducible blank grid which appears on page 77.

OPTIONAL ROLES AND AUDIENCES:

Ellen
the Giraffe
Kirsti
Papa
Peter
Uncle Henrick
King Christian
Nazi soldiers

OPTIONAL FORMATS AND STRONG VERBS:

short story / enlighten
fairy tale / explain
message / divulge
instructions / direct
proclamation / announce

OPTIONAL TOPICS:

what it's like without butter, sugar, and other basics

help Kirsti understand the soldier's presence

the safe arrivals of the Rosens and others

how to use the handkerchiefs without suspicion

Out of the Dust

by Karen Hesse

Newbery Award 1998

In this book of free verse poems, 14-year-old narrator Billie Jo Kelby tells stories of life in the Oklahoma dust bowl during the mid-1930s. Billie Jo reveals the happy times of her young adulthood along with the grim realities of living through constant dust storms, facing the death of her mother, and watching her father's decaying health. After escaping the dust on a westbound train, Billie Jo learns that getting away doesn't make life any better . . . just different.

R.A.F.T.S. PROMPT FILLED-IN GRID:

Role: Billie Jo

Audience: yourself

Format: two free-verse poems

Topic: why your family stays in Oklahoma

Strong Verbs: explain/share

R.A.F.T.S. PROMPT IN PARAGRAPH FORM:

You are <u>Billie Jo</u> and wonder <u>why your family stays in Oklahoma</u> after the death of
    (Role) and (Audience)   **(Topic)**
your mother. Create <u>two free-verse poems</u> to help you work out these feelings. In
                (Format)
the first, <u>explain</u> all the reasons you think you should stay, and in the second, <u>share</u>
  (Strong verb)   **(Strong verb)**
all the reasons you think you should go away from this harsh place.

Copy and distribute the reproducible R.A.F.T.S. prompt for *Out of the Dust,* found on page 71. You or your students can adapt this prompt or create additional ones by choosing components from the lists below or by brainstorming your own, then filling in a reproducible blank grid which appears on page 77.

OPTIONAL ROLES AND AUDIENCES:	**OPTIONAL FORMATS AND STRONG VERBS:**	**OPTIONAL TOPICS:**
Ma	free form verse / describe	how it felt to leave
Daddy	telegram / inform	Billie Jo's and Mad Dog's performance at the Palace Theater
Mr. Hardly	brochure / invite	
Livie	biographical sketch / reflect	Ma's life and death
Arley	encyclopedia entry / communicate	life in the Oklahoma dust bowl
Mad Dog		the birth of the new baby
Louise		
Doc Rice		

The Midwife's Apprentice
by Karen Cushman

Newbery Award 1996

It's fourteenth-century England, and a homeless waif of a girl is trying to survive any way she can. Jane, a midwife, finds her in a dung heap trying to stay warm, aptly names her Beetle, and takes her in as a helper. By observing the midwife and learning the spells and potions necessary to bring a child into the world, Beetle takes a journey from being a nobody to being a person with a place in the world.

R.A.F.T.S. PROMPT FILLED-IN GRID:

Role: Beetle

Audience: yourself

Format: diary entry

Topic: how you might escape being constantly teased by the village boys

Strong Verb: outline

R.A.F.T.S. PROMPT IN PARAGRAPH FORM:

You are <u>Beetle</u> and are tired of being teased as you walk through the village. Write a
    (Role) and (Audience)
<u>diary entry</u> <u>outlining</u> <u>how you might escape being constantly teased by the village boys</u>.
 (Format)   **(Strong verb)**   **(Topic)**
Be sure to mention the times and places when you think you'll need a good plan.

Copy and distribute the reproducible R.A.F.T.S. prompt for *The Midwife's Apprentice*, found on page 71. You or your students can adapt this prompt or create additional ones by choosing components from the lists below or by brainstorming your own, then filling in a reproducible blank grid which appears on page 77.

OPTIONAL ROLES AND AUDIENCES:

Jane
Will
Runt/Edward
women in the village
John Dark
Richard Reese
Purr

OPTIONAL FORMATS AND STRONG VERBS:

speech / dispell
letter of introduction / relate
journal entry / describe
instructions / teach
short story / moralize

OPTIONAL TOPICS:

the rumors about Jane's errands
the trip to Gobnet-Under-Green
Alyce's devil trick
how to bring a baby along faster
never giving up on what you
    really want

The Watsons Go to Birmingham—1963
by Christopher Paul Curtis

Newbery Honor 1996

Meet the fascinating Watson family of Flynt, Michigan, as seen through the eyes of ten-year-old Kenny. Momma, Dad, older brother Byron, Kenny, and sister Joetta live a life filled with funny family stories. But then Byron starts getting into serious trouble, forcing Momma and Dad to do something drastic: They drive him to Birmingham to live with his Grandma Sands for the summer. The trip brings the Watsons face-to-face with segregation and all of its ugliness, violence, and tragedy.

R.A.F.T.S. PROMPT FILLED-IN GRID:

Role: Kenny

Audience: the family

Format: story

Topic: your version of what happened that morning

Strong Verb: relate

R.A.F.T.S. PROMPT IN PARAGRAPH FORM:

You are <u>Kenny</u>. At dinner, you want to tell <u>the family</u> <u>your version of what happened</u>
     (Role)   **(Audience)**   **(Topic)**

<u>that morning</u> at the church. Write the <u>story</u> you plan to <u>relate</u>, being sure to include
                                             (Format)   **(Strong verb)**

your personal observations and insights about the bombing and how it will affect

your family and community.

Copy and distribute the reproducible R.A.F.T.S. prompt for *The Watsons Go to Birmingham—1963*, found on page 71. You or your students can adapt this prompt or create additional ones by choosing components from the lists below or by brainstorming your own, then filling in a reproducible blank grid which appears on page 77.

OPTIONAL ROLES AND AUDIENCES:	**OPTIONAL FORMATS AND STRONG VERBS:**	**OPTIONAL TOPICS:**
Momma	journal entry / scrutinize	getting teased at school
Dad	speech / confess	making amends with Rufus and Cody
Byron	legend / embellish	swimming at Collier's Landing
Joetta	historical account / express	the bomb
Grandma Sands	short story / explain	Joetta's helping ghost
Rufus		

The Whipping Boy

by Sid Fleischman

Newbery Award 1987

In Medieval times, an orphan and commoner named Jemmy is taken to the king's palace to become the whipping boy for Prince Brat, whose numerous tricks tempt Jemmy to escape. But Prince Brat beats him to it and escapes the palace himself, forcing Jemmy to go with him. What follows is a tale of mistaken identity, prince-nappers, thieves, and a dancing bear, as Prince Brat and Jemmy find their way back to the palace with valuable lessons learned and a brand new friendship.

R.A.F.T.S. PROMPT FILLED-IN GRID:

Role: Jemmy

Audience: Prince Brat

Format: plea

Topic: go along with your plan to trick the prince-nappers

Strong Verb: request

R.A.F.T.S. PROMPT IN PARAGRAPH FORM:

When Hold-Your-Nose Billy and Cutwater think you and the prince have changed

places, a plan pops into your head. As <u>Jemmy</u>, write the urgent <u>plea</u> you might
                                  (Role)   **(Format)**

present to the reluctant <u>Prince Brat</u>, to <u>request</u> that he <u>go along with your plan to</u>
                    (Audience)   **(Strong verb)**   **(Topic)**

<u>trick the prince-nappers</u>.

Copy and distribute the reproducible R.A.F.T.S. prompt for *The Whipping Boy*, found on page 72. You or your students can adapt this prompt or create additional ones by choosing components from the lists below or by brainstorming your own, then filling in a reproducible blank grid which appears on page 77.

OPTIONAL ROLES AND AUDIENCES:	**OPTIONAL FORMATS AND STRONG VERBS:**	**OPTIONAL TOPICS:**
Prince (Brat) Horace	short story / describe	the story of how Hold-Your-Nose Billy got his name
the king	wanted poster / identify	finding the prince-nappers
Master Peckwit	royal proclamation / declare	the whipping of the prince
Pa	commendation / thank	Petunia saves the day
Hold-Your-Nose Billy	song verses / characterize	new verses for the ballad of Hold-Your-Nose Billy
Cutwater		
Petunia		

The Winter Room

Newbery Honor 1990

by Gary Paulsen

Eleven-year-old Eldon narrates his view of 1930s family life on a Minnesota farm. He fondly remembers the sounds, the smells, and the looks of each season—especially those connected to the winter room, the family gathering place on cold winter evenings. Eldon, brother Wayne, Uncle Nels, Mom, and Dad all gather 'round to hear Uncle David tell his well-worn stories. But one special story, "The Woodcutter," leads Eldon and Wayne on a journey of discovery about their Uncle David and themselves.

R.A.F.T.S. PROMPT FILLED-IN GRID:

Role: Eldon

Audience: Mrs. Halverson

Format: poem

Topic: your favorite season on the farm

Strong Verb: describe

R.A.F.T.S. PROMPT IN PARAGRAPH FORM:

You are <u>Eldon</u> and you love all of the sights and sounds on the farm during the year.
       (Role)

Write a <u>poem</u> for <u>Mrs. Halverson</u> <u>describing</u> <u>your favorite season on the farm</u>. With
       (Format)   **(Audience)**   **(Strong verb)**   **(Topic)**

your poem, paint a picture of that season using as many sensory words as you can.

Copy and distribute the reproducible R.A.F.T.S. prompt for *The Winter Room*, found on page 72. You or your students can adapt this prompt or create additional ones by choosing components from the lists below or by brainstorming your own, then filling in a reproducible blank grid which appears on page 77.

OPTIONAL ROLES AND AUDIENCES:

Mom
Father
Wayne
Uncle David
Uncle Nels
Stacker
Mrs. Halverson
Eldon

OPTIONAL FORMATS AND STRONG VERBS:

short story / detail
diary entry / describe
advertisement / convince
dialogue / embellish
skit / visualize

OPTIONAL TOPICS:

the meeting of Alida and Uncle David

the look and feel of the winter room

finding plow horses for the farm

the day Wayne jumped on Stacker's back

Ready-to-Use
R.A.F.T.S. Prompts

Fantasy

Fiction

Afternoon of the Elves

by Janet Taylor Lisle

Newbery
Honor
1990

Eleven-year-old Sara-Kate Connelly is a thin, unpopular girl who wins the friendship of nine-year-old Hillary Lennox with tales of a tiny elf village in her backyard. With Sara-Kate as the leader, the elf village brings magic into the new friendship and into their lives. But one day, Sara-Kate disappears and the elf village begins to fall into ruins. In an effort to save the elves' future, Hillary stumbles on the tragic truth about Sara-Kate and learns some hard lessons about friendship.

R.A.F.T.S. PROMPT FILLED-IN GRID:

Role: Hillary

Audience: Alison and Jane

Format: note

Topic: there is a real elf village in Sara-Kate's backyard

Strong Verb: convince

R.A.F.T.S. PROMPT IN PARAGRAPH FORM:

Your friends are concerned about your new friendship with Sara-Kate. As <u>Hillary,</u>
                                                                        (Role)
write a <u>note</u> you might pass to <u>Alison and Jane</u> at school to <u>convince</u> them that
       (Format)   **(Audience)**   **(Strong verb)**
<u>there is a real elf village in Sara-Kate's backyard</u>. Include several of the details about
                        (Topic)
the village that made you believe it was real.

Copy and distribute the reproducible R.A.F.T.S. prompt for *Afternoon of the Elves*, found on page 72. You or your students can adapt this prompt or create additional ones by choosing components from the lists below or by brainstorming your own, then filling in a reproducible blank grid which appears on page 77.

OPTIONAL ROLES AND AUDIENCES:	**OPTIONAL FORMATS AND STRONG VERBS:**	**OPTIONAL TOPICS:**
Sara-Kate	list / identify	the building of the ferris wheel
Alison	encyclopedia entry / define	the characteristics of elves
Jane	invitation / request	joining the elves in an elf banquet
Mrs. Lennox	diary entry / confess	whether Sara-Kate was truly an elf or just a girl
Mr. Lennox	debate / analyze	
Hillary		

Gathering Blue
by Lois Lowry

K ira, a recently orphaned young girl who is plagued by a deformed leg, tries to find her place in a society that shuns the weak. When she is taken to The Council of Guardians to face judgment, she is given a reprieve because of her artistic skill in threadwork and is asked to live in the grand Council Edifice as a resident artist. While there, Kira and her fellow artists learn the importance of tradition and the secrets of the Ruin Song.

R.A.F.T.S. PROMPT FILLED-IN GRID:

Role: Matt

Audience: Kira

Format: set of directions

Topic: your journey to the village of the healing

Strong Verb: reconstruct

R.A.F.T.S. PROMPT IN PARAGRAPH FORM:

You are <u>Matt</u> and you're getting ready to guide Kira's father back home. Write
      (Role)

a <u>set of directions</u> for <u>Kira</u> that <u>reconstructs</u> <u>your journey to the village of the healing</u>,
  (Format)   **(Audience)**   **(Strong verb)**   **(Topic)**

so she may follow it if she wishes to see her father. Include some important

landmarks to serve as guideposts along the way.

Copy and distribute the reproducible R.A.F.T.S. prompt for *Gathering Blue*, found on page 72. You or your students can adapt this prompt or create additional ones by choosing components from the lists below or by brainstorming your own, then filling in a reproducible blank grid which appears on page 77.

OPTIONAL ROLES AND AUDIENCES:	OPTIONAL FORMATS AND STRONG VERBS:	OPTIONAL TOPICS:
Kira	diary entry / lament	your mother and the leaving field
Katrina	summary / compare	Kira's cot and her new room at the Council Edifice
Vandara	list / describe	
Jamison	brochure / exemplify	Annabelle's plants and colors
Thomas	letter / confide	the beauty of the Singer's robe
the Singer		Kira's duty to her village

Harry Potter and the Sorcerer's Stone
by J. K. Rowling

In this first of five books in the popular fantasy series, young Harry Potter discovers his true identity as a wizard who is revered throughout the wizard world. He is the only known survivor of Lord Voldemort's wrath, and wizards everywhere await in terror what might happen when Harry and Lord Voldemort meet again. Meanwhile, Harry's days at Hogwarts school are filled with flying Quiddich matches, potions classes, magical meals and passages, and adventures with his new best friends Ron Weasley, Hermione Granger, and the giant Hagrid.

R.A.F.T.S. PROMPT FILLED-IN GRID:

Role: Hagrid

Audience: Professor Dumbledore

Format: conversation

Topic: several different things you will do to keep Harry Potter safe

Strong Verb: reflect

R.A.F.T.S. PROMPT IN PARAGRAPH FORM:

You are the giant, <u>Hagrid</u>, from Hogwarts. In a <u>conversation</u> with <u>Professor</u>
            (Role)   **(Format)**

<u>Dumbledore</u>, <u>reflect</u> on <u>several different things you will do to keep Harry Potter safe</u>
  (Audience)   **(Strong verb)**   **(Topic)**

once he arrives at school and begins his classes. Since Lord Voldemort will not stay

silent once he learns that Harry has come of age, be sure to include ways that Harry

can protect himself from the Dark Lord, too.

Copy and distribute the reproducible R.A.F.T.S. prompt for *Harry Potter and the Sorcerer's Stone*, found on page 72. You or your students can adapt this prompt or create additional ones by choosing components from the lists below or by brainstorming your own, then filling in a reproducible blank grid which appears on page 77.

OPTIONAL ROLES AND AUDIENCES:	**OPTIONAL FORMATS AND STRONG VERBS:**	**OPTIONAL TOPICS:**
the Dursleys	description / characterize	how Bertie Bott's Every Flavor Beans taste
the Sorting Hat	spells / clarify	step-by-step directions for a spell
Professor McGonagall	research paper / report	how to play Quiddich
Professor Dumbledore	rules / relate	a map of Hogwarts and all of its rooms
Fluffy	map / divulge	

James and the Giant Peach
by Roald Dahl

James Henry Trotter loses his parents in a terrible rhinoceros accident and is sent to live with his wicked Aunt Sponge and Aunt Spiker. Unbearably lonely and sad, he finds solace in a bag of magic green "things" given to him by an old man. When James accidentally spills the green things in the garden near the peach tree, a single large peach miraculously grows. One day, James climbs into the giant peach, meets amazing new friends, and rolls away from his unhappiness into a whole new life.

R.A.F.T.S. PROMPT FILLED-IN GRID:

Role: James

Audience: Aunt Sponge and Aunt Spiker

Format: good-bye note

Topic: your reasons for leaving

Strong Verb: defend

R.A.F.T.S. PROMPT IN PARAGRAPH FORM:

You are <u>James</u> and you know it is time to leave your aunts' house. Write a <u>good-bye</u>
      (Role)
<u>note</u> to <u>Aunt Sponge and Aunt Spiker</u> before you climb into the giant peach. In your
(Format)   **(Audience)**
note, <u>defend</u> <u>your reasons for leaving</u> so that they will really understand.
    (Strong verb)   **(Topic)**

Copy and distribute the reproducible R.A.F.T.S. prompt for *James and the Giant Peach*, found on page 73. You or your students can adapt this prompt or create additional ones by choosing components from the lists below or by brainstorming your own, then filling in a reproducible blank grid which appears on page 77.

OPTIONAL ROLES AND AUDIENCES:	OPTIONAL FORMATS AND STRONG VERBS:	OPTIONAL TOPICS:
Aunt Sponge	journal entry / reflect	what it might have been like to go down off the top of the hill and play
Aunt Spiker	list / describe	
the old man	fairy tale / imagine	a day of chores given to you by Aunt Sponge and Aunt Spiker
Old-Green Grasshopper	instructions / inform	
Spider	television announcement / convince	what might have happened if James had put the little green things in the jug of water
Ladybug		
Centipede		
Earthworm		

Matilda

by Roald Dahl

Matilda Wormwood—supernerd, genius, and teacher's pet—not only has the most self-centered parents she knows, but also the most nightmarish school principal on earth, Mrs. Trunchbull. Intelligent and patient Matilda reaches deep for ways to deal with these annoyances, resulting in practical jokes and revenge. The true test comes when Matilda decides to defend her teacher against "The Trunchbull" and discovers something new about herself.

R.A.F.T.S. PROMPT FILLED-IN GRID:

Role: Matilda

Audience: Miss Honey

Format: diary entry

Topic: how you feel before, during, and after you move things with your mind

Strong Verb: examine

R.A.F.T.S. PROMPT IN PARAGRAPH FORM:

You are <u>Matilda</u> and you are interested in everything about your new psychic gift.
        (Role) and (Audience)

Write a <u>diary entry</u> <u>examining</u> <u>how you feel before, during, and after you move things</u>
        (Format)   **(Strong verb)**   **(Topic)**

<u>with your mind</u>. Use lots of details to describe your sensory experiences.

Copy and distribute the reproducible R.A.F.T.S. prompt for *Matilda*, found on page 73. You or your students can adapt this prompt or create additional ones by choosing components from the lists below or by brainstorming your own, then filling in a reproducible blank grid which appears on page 77.

OPTIONAL ROLES AND AUDIENCES:	OPTIONAL FORMATS AND STRONG VERBS:	OPTIONAL TOPICS:
Lavender	short story / visualize	the reading room
Miss Honey	fable / moralize	teaching Mr. Wormwood a lesson
children in Matilda's class	legend / relate	the Chokey
Matilda's parents	commentary / illuminate	why the students are afraid of "The Trunchbull"
Miss Trunchbull	letter / describe	
Magnus		new life with Miss Honey

Midnight Magic
by Avi

*S*et in the imaginary kingdom of Pergamontio in 1491, this story reveals a ghostly conspiracy involving the weak King Claudio, the unpredictable Princess Teresina, the conniving Queen Jovanna, the diabolical Count Scarazoni, the skeptical Magnus the Magician, and his gullible servant, Fabrizio. By traveling the secret halls and chambers of the dark and moldy castello, Fabrizio and Magnus uncover the story of the ghost and its connection to the royal family.

R.A.F.T.S. PROMPT FILLED-IN GRID:

Role: Count Scarazoni

Audience: Princess Teresina

Format: announcement

Topic: your intentions to marry her, ghost or no ghost

Strong Verb: inform

R.A.F.T.S. PROMPT IN PARAGRAPH FORM:

You are <u>Count Scarazoni</u> and you realize that this ghost may stop you from attaining
            (Role)

your goals. Write an <u>announcement</u> to give before <u>Princess Teresina</u> <u>informing</u> her of
                          (Format)   **(Audience)**   **(Strong verb)**

<u>your intentions to marry her, ghost or no ghost</u>. Include at least three reasons for her
                          (Topic)

to believe it will happen.

Copy and distribute the reproducible R.A.F.T.S. prompt for *Midnight Magic*, found on page 73. You or your students can adapt this prompt or create additional ones by choosing components from the lists below or by brainstorming your own, then filling in a reproducible blank grid which appears on page 77.

OPTIONAL ROLES AND AUDIENCES:	OPTIONAL FORMATS AND STRONG VERBS:	OPTIONAL TOPICS:
Fabrizio	biographical sketch / characterize	how Fabrizio learned so many sayings
Magnus the Magician	anecdote / contemplate	why Magnus does not believe in magic
King Claudio	directions / describe	
Queen Jovanna	dialogue / confide	the scheme of creating a ghost
Princess Teresina	announcement / clarify	the death of the prince on the road to Rome
Rinaldo		
Count Scarazoni		

The Book of Three

by Lloyd Alexander

•————•————•

While searching for Hen Wen, the ocular pig who has escaped into the woods, Taran, the pig's keeper, finds himself on a mission to save the land of Prydain from evil. Along the way, Taran meets up with Prince Gwydion and the pair travels together seeking the knowledgeable pig. The journey brings an assortment of companions—the hungry forest creature Gurgi, the courageous Eilonwy, the bard Fflewddur Fflam, and the dwarf Doli of the Fair Folk—who help Taran on his mission to warn the Sons of Don about the sinister plans for Prydain.

R.A.F.T.S. PROMPT FILLED-IN GRID:

Role: Prince Gwydion

Audience: your companions (Fflewddur Fflam, Doli, Gurgi, Eilonwy, and Taran)

Format: royal proclamation

Topic: gifts you will bestow upon each of them for their bravery

Strong Verb: announce

R.A.F.T.S. PROMPT IN PARAGRAPH FORM:

You are <u>Prince Gwydion</u> and you have summoned all of your companions to the
           (Role)

Great Hall of Caer Dathyl. Write a <u>royal proclamation</u> to deliver to <u>Fflewddur Fflam,</u>
                                        (Format)   (Audience)

<u>Doli, Gurgi, Eilonwy, and Taran, announcing</u> the <u>gifts you will bestow upon each of</u>
                              (Strong verb)   (Topic)

<u>them for their bravery</u>.

Copy and distribute the reproducible R.A.F.T.S. prompt for *The Book of Three*, found on page 73. You or your students can adapt this prompt or create additional ones by choosing components from the lists below or by brainstorming your own, then filling in a reproducible blank grid which appears on page 77.

OPTIONAL ROLES AND AUDIENCES:	OPTIONAL FORMATS AND STRONG VERBS:	OPTIONAL TOPICS:
Taran	legend / visualize	the story of Achren's sword
Coll	plan / construct	getting weapons from the Spiral Castle
Dallben	commentary / confess	
Horned King	instructions/ divulge	Taran's decision not to leave Gurgi behind
Hen Wen	short story / illuminate	
Eilonwy		the healing of Gurgi
Achren		what happened to Achren
The Cauldron-Born		

The Indian in the Cupboard
by Lynne Reid Banks

I t's Omri's birthday and he's thrilled with the old medicine cupboard that his brother Gillon gives him as a gift. But he's not so thrilled with the second-hand plastic Indian figure he gets from his best friend Patrick. Then Omri places the figure in the cupboard and locks it away with an old key belonging to his grandmother. With a turn of the key, the Indian figure magically turns into a tiny living being and Omri learns about the responsibilities of friendship, caring, and letting go.

R.A.F.T.S. PROMPT FILLED-IN GRID:

Role: Iroquois elder

Audience: Omri

Format: old Indian legend

Topic: how the Indian wound up in the cupboard

Strong Verb: reveal

R.A.F.T.S. PROMPT IN PARAGRAPH FORM:

You are an <u>Iroquois elder</u> and Little Bear has asked you to explain to <u>Omri</u>
          (Role)   (Audience)
how a tiny Indian can mysteriously appear. Create an <u>old Indian legend</u> to <u>reveal</u>
                                                      (Format)   (Strong verb)
<u>how the Indian wound up in the cupboard</u>.
          (Topic)

Copy and distribute the reproducible R.A.F.T.S. prompt for *The Indian in the Cupboard*, found on page 73. You or your students can adapt this prompt or create additional ones by choosing components from the lists below or by brainstorming your own, then filling in a reproducible blank grid which appears on page 77.

OPTIONAL ROLES AND AUDIENCES:	OPTIONAL FORMATS AND STRONG VERBS:	OPTIONAL TOPICS:
Omri	historical account / relate	the forming of a friendship and earning trust
Patrick	telephone conversation / divulge	
Gillon	commentary / define	sharing the secret of the tiny Indian
Adiel	step-by-step directions / describe	
Little Bear	letter / reflect	enemies becoming blood brothers
Tommy		
Boone		saying good-bye and returning the figures to the cupboard

The Little Prince

by Antoine de Saint-Exupéry

First published in 1943, The Little Prince *was originally written in French and has been translated into many languages. The story is narrated by a pilot whose airplane goes down in the Sahara Desert. While trying to repair it, he meets a little prince from Asteroid B-612, who asks him to draw a sheep. Although surprised and confused, the pilot takes a scrap of paper and pencil and does what he is told, beginning a dialogue that touches on tiny worlds, simple flowers, children, the strangeness of grown-ups, loneliness, solitude, and what is really important in life.*

R.A.F.T.S. PROMPT FILLED-IN GRID:

Role: the Little Prince

Audience: pilot

Format: travelogue entries

Topic: the strangeness of adults on the planets you visit

Strong Verb: describe

R.A.F.T.S. PROMPT IN PARAGRAPH FORM:

You are <u>the Little Prince</u> and you have visited seven planets and talked with several
      (Role)
adults. Write the <u>travelogue entries</u> that you might have kept for the <u>pilot, describing</u>
      (Format)   **(Audience)**   **(Strong verb)**
<u>the strangeness of the adults on the planets you visit</u>.
      (Topic)

Copy and distribute the reproducible R.A.F.T.S. prompt for *The Little Prince*, found on page 73. You or your students can adapt this prompt or create additional ones by choosing components from the lists below or by brainstorming your own, then filling in a reproducible blank grid which appears on page 77.

OPTIONAL ROLES AND AUDIENCES:	**OPTIONAL FORMATS AND STRONG VERBS:**	**OPTIONAL TOPICS:**
pilot	advertisement / encourage	growing roses on B-612 and on Earth
flower	debate / analyze	the beauty of sunsets on B-612
king	encyclopedia entry / define	the taming of the fox
vain man	set of instructions / inform	what's important is invisible
drunkard	fable / moralize	the difference between owning and reigning over
businessman		
old geographer		

The Moorchild

by Eloise McGraw

This is the extraordinary tale of Moql, a young girl who is half human and half Folk, the elf-like people who live on the moor. Although she was raised by Folk, Moql is eventually forced from the moor and into the human world as a "changeling" child, and renamed Saaski. From the very beginning, Saaski knows she is different from the other children, but is never quite sure why until she encounters the Moorfolk, learns of her past, and makes her own way in the world.

R.A.F.T.S. PROMPT FILLED-IN GRID:

Role: Saaski

Audience: Anwara and Yanno

Format: poem

Topic: times you felt that strange feeling of love

Strong Verb: describe

R.A.F.T.S. PROMPT IN PARAGRAPH FORM:

You are <u>Saaski</u>. Write a <u>poem</u> to <u>Anwara and Yanno</u> <u>describing</u> the <u>times you felt that</u>
      (Role)   (Format)   (Audience)   (Strong verb)   (Topic)
<u>strange feeling of love</u> while growing up in their household. In your poem, include

at least two situations when you felt their love for you and two situations when you

felt love for them.

Copy and distribute the reproducible R.A.F.T.S. prompt for *The Moorchild*, found on page 74. You or your students can adapt this prompt or create additional ones by choosing components from the lists below or by brainstorming your own, then filling in a reproducible blank grid which appears on page 77.

OPTIONAL ROLES AND AUDIENCES:	OPTIONAL FORMATS AND STRONG VERBS:	OPTIONAL TOPICS:
Old Bess	instructions / teach	how changelings came to be
Anwara	legend / narrate	the folk runes that only Folk can see
Yanno	dictionary entries / define	
Moql	journal entry / relate	what it's like to meet your real mother and father
Pittittiskin	discussion / gossip	
Tarabar		Saaski's unusual behavior at home and in the town
Fergil		

The Phantom Tollbooth

by Norton Juster

O ne day, Milo, a bored child who is having trouble seeing the use in anything, finds a mysterious box in his bedroom. Since Milo has nothing better to do with his time, he opens the box to find parts of a tollbooth and directions for assembling it. Once construction is complete, Milo drives his car through the tollbooth and begins a journey to wonderfully wordy Dictionopolis and beyond, encountering a host of interesting characters who lead him to become a hero and rescue the princesses Rhyme and Reason from the Castle in the Air.

R.A.F.T.S. PROMPT FILLED-IN GRID:

Role: Tock

Audience: Milo

Format: daily schedule

Topic: a typical day in Dictionopolis, where no time is wasted and
no alarm sounds

Strong Verb: describe

R.A.F.T.S. PROMPT IN PARAGRAPH FORM:

Tock hates to waste time. In fact, if he wastes time, an alarm goes off on the

clock in his stomach. As <u>Tock</u>, write a <u>daily schedule</u> to share with <u>Milo</u> <u>describing</u>
         (Role)   **(Format)**   **(Audience)** **(Strong verb)**
<u>a typical day in Dictionopolis, where no time is wasted and no alarm sounds</u>.
         (Topic)

Copy and distribute the reproducible R.A.F.T.S. prompt for *The Phantom Tollbooth*, found on page 74. You or your students can adapt this prompt or create additional ones by choosing components from the lists below or by brainstorming your own, then filling in a reproducible blank grid which appears on page 77.

OPTIONAL ROLES AND AUDIENCES:	OPTIONAL FORMATS AND STRONG VERBS:	OPTIONAL TOPICS:
Milo	skit / describe	when all talk stopped in Dictionopolis
Whether Man	brochure / convince	musical sunsets
The Doldrums	legend / relate	how the city of words got its name
Lethargarians	debate / express	
King Azaz	newspaper article / communicate	numbers are more important than words in Digitopolis
Spelling Bee		
Humbug		
Officer Short Shrift		the rescue of Rhyme and Reason

The Spiderwick Chronicles, Book 1: The Field Guide
by Holly Black and Tony DiTerlizzi

This is the first installment in a series of five books. Mallory, Simon, and Jared Grace find themselves living in a new town, in an old and decrepit Victorian house that gives them and their newly divorced mom a real fright. The siblings discover secret rooms, strange goings on, and an old book, Arthur Spiderwick's Field Guide to the Fantastical World Around You. With an ominous warning from a not-so-friendly boggart, the kids embark on a search to reveal the mysteries of the old house.

R.A.F.T.S. PROMPT FILLED-IN GRID:

Role: Jared

Audience: Simon and Mallory

Format: map

Topic: the secret room of Arthur Spiderwick

Strong Verb: explore

R.A.F.T.S. PROMPT IN PARAGRAPH FORM:

You are <u>Jared</u> and you have discovered the secret room in the attic once occupied
    (Role)
by an old relative, Arthur Spiderwick. Create a <u>map</u> of the house with directions for
            (Format)
<u>exploring</u> <u>the secret room of Arthur Spiderwick</u>, so <u>Simon and Mallory</u> can join you
  (Strong verb)   **(Topic)**   **(Audience)**
as you investigate all the secrets of this mysterious place.

Copy and distribute the reproducible R.A.F.T.S. prompt for *The Spiderwick Chronicles, Book 1: The Field Guide*, found on page 74. You or your students can adapt this prompt or create additional ones by choosing components from the lists below or by brainstorming your own, then filling in a reproducible blank grid which appears on page 77.

OPTIONAL ROLES AND AUDIENCES:

Great Aunt Lucinda
Uncle Arthur
former classmates and friends
the fairies
neighbors
newspaper reporters

OPTIONAL FORMATS AND STRONG VERBS:

newspaper article / describe
letters to friends / explain
phone conversations with Dad / list
illustrations with captions / visualize
diary entry / expand

OPTIONAL TOPICS:

Mrs. Grace's diary of the first days in the old house

Aunt Lucinda's warnings about the house

everything that has to be fixed around the old house

what does a boggart look like?

Tuck Everlasting

by Natalie Babbitt

Ten-year-old Winnie Foster decides to run away from home. At the start of her journey, in the woods of her family's property, she stumbles onto Jesse Tuck drinking from a spring near a large tree and soon learns that the spring has given everlasting life not only to him, but to his family members Mae, Miles, and Angus Tuck. In order to protect the magic of the spring, Winnie travels with the Tucks to their home and learns that things are not as simple as they seem. The choice of everlasting life is a difficult one.

R.A.F.T.S. PROMPT FILLED-IN GRID:

Role: Winnie

Audience: Disney Studio executives

Format: lyrics for a song

Topic: the miracle of everlasting life

Strong Verb: extol

R.A.F.T.S. PROMPT IN PARAGRAPH FORM:

The <u>Disney Studio executives</u> are looking for a theme song for the new movie
(Audience)

version of *Tuck Everlasting*. As <u>Winnie</u>, compose the <u>lyrics for a song</u> that <u>extol</u>
(Role)   (Format)   (Strong verb)

<u>the miracle of everlasting life.</u>
(Topic)

Copy and distribute the reproducible R.A.F.T.S. prompt for *Tuck Everlasting*, found on page 74. You or your students can adapt this prompt or create additional ones by choosing components from the lists below or brainstorming your own, then filling in a reproducible blank grid which appears on page 77.

OPTIONAL ROLES AND AUDIENCES:	**OPTIONAL FORMATS AND STRONG VERBS:**	**OPTIONAL TOPICS:**
Mrs. Foster	advertisement / encourage	the question of selling the spring water
Mr. Foster	marriage proposal / convince	
Mae	debate / decide	Jesse's marriage proposal
Tuck	short story / predict	Mae and the murder
Miles	dialogue / relate	Winnie's decision about everlasting life
Jesse		
Granny		Jesse's final good-bye to Winnie

Walk Two Moons

by Sharon Creech

Newbery
Award
1995

Salamanca Tree Hiddle's mother, Chanhassen, has gone away, leaving her confused and her father unhappy. They find little comfort in the postcards she sends, marking her trip across the country. But then one day the postcards stop. To work out her feelings of her mother's abandonment, Salamanca takes a road trip across the country with her grandparents. Salamanca learns a lot about herself, her mother, and her grandparents from her story-telling trip, and she finds the answer to the mystery of why her mother never returned.

R.A.F.T.S. PROMPT FILLED-IN GRID:

Role: Chanhassen

Audience: Salamanca and her father

Format: post cards with illustrations

Topic: where you have gone

Strong Verb: determine

R.A.F.T.S. PROMPT IN PARAGRAPH FORM:

You are <u>Chanhassen</u>, who has left home without explanation. Write a series of <u>post</u>
      (Role)
<u>cards with illustrations</u> from all the places you go to send to <u>Salamanca and her</u>
      (Format)   **(Audience)**
<u>father</u> so they have a few clues to <u>determine</u> <u>where you have gone</u>. Include the
                                (Strong verb)   **(Topic)**
reasons why you stopped at each place to provide your family with information to

help them understand your actions.

Copy and distribute the reproducible R.A.F.T.S. prompt for *Walk Two Moons*, found on page 74. You or your students can adapt this prompt or create additional ones by choosing components from the lists below or by brainstorming your own, then filling in a reproducible blank grid which appears on page 77.

OPTIONAL ROLES AND AUDIENCES:	**OPTIONAL FORMATS AND STRONG VERBS:**	**OPTIONAL TOPICS:**
Salamanca	diary entry / define	the mystery of the envelopes being placed on the front porch
Father	telephone conversation / scrutinize	kissing trees all over the town
Margaret	legend / explain	walking in someone else's moccasins
Phoebe	short story / empathize	
Gram		

REALISTIC FICTION

Bridge to Terabithia by Katherine Paterson

You are <u>Jess Aarons</u> and your sister, May Belle, keeps asking to go with you to Terabithia. Write
      (Role)

<u>a letter</u> to <u>May Belle</u>, <u>explaining</u> <u>several good reasons why she may not swing on the magic rope to</u>
(Format)   **(Audience)**   **(Strong verb)**   **(Topic)**
<u>Terabithia</u> with you and Leslie.

Dear Mr. Henshaw by Beverly Cleary

You are <u>Leigh</u> and are very upset after talking to your dad on the telephone. Not only had he not
      (Role)

called in a while, but when he finally did, you heard a woman and a boy in the background. Write

an <u>e-mail</u> to your <u>best friend</u> <u>sharing</u> your <u>feelings about your conversation with your father</u>.
 (Format)   **(Audience) (Strong verb)**   **(Topic)**

Everything on a Waffle by Polly Horvath

You are <u>Primrose Squarp</u>. Create a waffle <u>menu</u> for <u>restaurant patrons</u> <u>describing</u>
      (Role)   **(Format)**   **(Audience)**   **(Strong verb)**
<u>the most appetizing of Kate's famous dishes</u>. Don't forget to include the regular selections,
    (Topic)

dieter's selections, and children's selections on your menu.

Fig Pudding by Ralph Fletcher

<u>Teddy's brothers</u> find it amusing that he spends all of his time under the kitchen table.
    (Role)
<u>Capture</u> <u>Teddy's mood and reasons for his decision to park himself under the table</u> through a
(Strong verb)   **(Topic)**

<u>series of illustrations with captions</u> to amuse <u>Mom and Dad</u>. Organize the series on a storyboard
      (Format)   **(Audience)**

for presentation.

Frindle by Andrew Clements

You are <u>one of the students in Nick's classroom</u>. Thanks to Nick, you have a new word in your
(Role)
vocabulary. As an assignment for <u>Mrs. Granger</u>, write the complete, <u>unabridged dictionary entry,</u>
(Audience)   (Format)
<u>defining</u> the word *frindle* <u>and all of its possible meanings.</u>
(Strong verb)   (Topic)

- -

From the Mixed-up Files of Mrs. Basil E. Frankweiler by E. L. Konigsburg

You are <u>E. L. Konigsburg</u>, the author of this wonderful book. Write a <u>memo</u> that you will share with
(Role)   (Format)
<u>your publisher</u> at an editorial meeting, <u>persuading</u> him to <u>use the title you have selected over the</u>
(Audience)   (Strong verb)   (Topic)
<u>three other possible titles</u> that he likes better.

- -

Harris and Me: A Summer Remembered by Gary Paulsen

You are <u>Harris</u> and you think it is fun to make your citified cousin look silly. Write a <u>set of</u>
(Role)   (Format)
<u>instructions</u> to <u>hoodwink</u> <u>your cousin</u> into thinking that <u>Ernie, the rooster, can be caught and put</u>
(Strong verb) (Audience)   (Topic)
<u>into his coop at the end of the day.</u> Be sure to include the reason behind each step of the

instructions.

- -

Hatchet by Gary Paulsen

You are <u>Brian</u> after your perilous experience. Write a <u>chapter of a survival handbook,</u> <u>outlining</u>
(Role)   (Format)   (Strong verb)
<u>the key survival techniques you learned in the Canadian wilderness</u> that <u>anyone who might ever be</u>
(Topic)   (Audience)
<u>stranded</u> should know. Focus on food, shelter, or protection.

- -

Holes by Louis Sachar

You are <u>Stanley</u> and you want to make sure that <u>you and Zero</u> can find <u>the location of the hole</u>
(Role)   (Audience)
<u>where the mysterious tube was found.</u> Draw a <u>secret map</u> of Camp Green Lake with all the holes
(Topic)   (Format)
labeled with the names of the people who dug them to help you <u>identify</u> the actual hole in which
(Strong verb)
the tube was found.

Hoot by Carl Hiaasen

You are <u>Roy Eberhardt and/or Beatrice Leap</u> of Coconut Grove, Florida. In a front page
(Role)
<u>newspaper article</u> for the <u>people of Coconut Grove,</u> <u>clarify</u> <u>why Mother Paula's All-American</u>
(Format)   (Audience)   (Strong verb)   (Topic)
<u>Pancake House is moving its building site</u> from its original location to the corner of East Oriole

and Woodbury.

How to Eat Fried Worms by Thomas Rockwell

You are <u>Mrs. Forester</u> and you realize that Billy will never win the bet for the $50.00 without your
(Role)
help. Write a <u>speech</u> to give to the <u>entire family,</u> <u>convincing</u> members that <u>eating your delicious</u>
(Format)   (Audience)   (Strong verb)
<u>new worm recipe for dinner will help Billy get the minibike.</u>
(Topic)

Maniac Magee by Jerry Spinelli

You are <u>Maniac Magee.</u> For a Christmas present, you give <u>Grayson</u> a short story you wrote about his
(Role)   (Audience)
baseball playing years, titled <u>*The Man Who Struck Out Willie Mays*</u>. <u>Write</u> the <u>first page of the story</u>.
(Topic)   (Strong verb)   (Format)
To hook the reader, include the most interesting things you know about Grayson.

Mick Harte Was Here by Barbara Park

You are <u>Mick's best friend</u> and have been asked to speak at his memorial service. Write the
(Role)
<u>eulogy</u> that you give at the service to help the grieving <u>family and friends</u> <u>remember</u>
(Format)   (Audience)   (Strong verb)
<u>all of the great things about Mick and his life</u>.
(Topic)

Tales of a Fourth Grade Nothing by Judy Blume

You are <u>Peter</u> and you want to amuse <u>your parents</u> with <u>some of the silly things your brother,</u>
(Role)   (Audience)   (Topic)
<u>Fudge, does</u>. In a <u>script for a skit</u> that you will perform, <u>characterize</u> some of Fudge's more zany
(Format)   (Strong verb)

antics.

Writing to Prompts in the Trait-Based Classroom: Literature Response Scholastic Teaching Resources

Tangerine by Edward Bloor

You are <u>Paul</u> and you have just been kicked off the soccer team. Write a <u>top-ten list</u> of your <u>skills</u>
    (Role) and (Audience)   (Format)
<u>and contributions as a soccer player, friend, family member, and citizen of the town of Tangerine</u>. In
                         (Topic)
your list, <u>examine</u> how your poor eyesight impacts people's perceptions of you and your skills and
    (Strong verb)
contributions.

- -

The Outsiders by S. E. Hinton

Darry and Ponyboy have been fighting ever since their parents died and Darry stepped in as head

of the family. As <u>Soda</u>, write a <u>speech</u> to <u>enlighten</u> <u>Darry and Ponyboy</u> about <u>what their fighting is</u>
             (Role)   (Format)   (Strong verb)   (Audience)   (Topic)
<u>doing to you and the family</u>. Include specific instances of their fighting and how they made you feel.

- -

The View from Saturday by E. L. Konigsburg

You are <u>Mrs. Olinski</u> and want <u>students, staff, and parents</u> to learn about the academic
       (Role)   (Audience)
team you have chosen. <u>Introduce</u> the members of the team through a <u>poster</u> that highlights
        (Strong verb)   (Format)
<u>the unique strengths and qualities of each person selected for the team</u>.
                  (Topic)

- -

What Jamie Saw by Carolyn Coman

As <u>Jamie</u>, write a <u>diary entry</u> to <u>explain</u> <u>how you feel about the night Van threw your baby sister, Nin</u>.
(Role) and (Audience)   (Format)   (Strong verb)   (Topic)
Be sure to include how you might tell your mom about your fears and concerns, without upsetting her

more than she already is.

- -

Where the Red Fern Grows: The Story of Two Dogs and a Boy by Wilson Rawls

You are the <u>breeder/owner</u> of some coonhound pups. Create an <u>advertisement</u> that will <u>advise</u>
    (Role)   (Format)   (Strong verb)
<u>prospective dog owners, including Grandpa</u>, of all the <u>information they need about your</u>
          (Audience)   (Topic)
<u>coonhound pups</u>. Be sure to include some good reasons to buy your pups instead of other

breeders'.

A Year Down Yonder by Richard Peck

You are <u>Grandma Dowdel</u> and you want Mary Alice to buy into <u>your new, wacky scheme to help</u>
     (Role)   **(Topic)**
<u>the town</u>. Write a <u>summary</u> of your scheme to <u>convince</u> <u>Mary Alice</u> that it's a good idea and that
          (Format)   **(Strong verb)** **(Audience)**
everything will turn out alright.

Across Five Aprils by Irene Hunt

You are <u>Bill</u> and have been told by your brother that the family is hearing a lot of unfavorable talk
     (Role)
about <u>your choice to fight for the South</u>. Write a <u>letter to the editor</u> of the local paper <u>defending</u>
        (Topic)   **(Format)**   **(Strong verb)**
your decision in hopes that <u>the townspeople</u> will read it and understand why you made this choice.
                    (Audience)

Bud, Not Buddy by Christopher Paul Curtis

As <u>Bud</u>, write a two-minute <u>plea</u> to be played on a local television station, <u>appealing</u> to <u>TV viewers</u>
    (Role)   **(Format)**   **(Strong verb)**   **(Audience)**
to contact you with <u>information that might lead to the discovery of the whereabouts of your dad,</u>
                                         (Topic)
<u>Herman E. Calloway</u>.

Crispin: The Cross of Lead by Avi

Although Father Quinel never got the opportunity to tell Crispin <u>who his mother and father really</u>
                                                          (Topic)
<u>were</u>, he had the speech all planned. Write this <u>speech</u>, <u>revealing</u> all of Crispin's family secrets, and
                                        (Format) **(Strong verb)**
deliver it the way <u>Father Quinel</u> would have to <u>Crispin</u>: through the window of the church
                    (Role)   **(Audience)**
confession booth.

Homeless Bird by Gloria Whelan

You are <u>Koly</u> and you realize you need to learn to support yourself now that you have been
     (Role)
abandoned by Sass. Write a <u>résumé</u> <u>highlighting</u> <u>your many skills, especially in embroidery,</u>
                 (Format)   **(Strong verb)**   **(Topic)**
to encourage a <u>prospective employer</u> to hire you.
         (Audience)

Homesick: My Own Story by Jean Fritz

As <u>Jean</u>, write a <u>letter</u> to <u>Grandma</u> to <u>convince</u> her that <u>talking your dad into coming back to</u>
  (Role)   (Format)   (Audience)   (Strong verb)   (Topic)

<u>America immediately</u> is a good idea. Include a couple of "narrow squeaks" that will help drive
      (Topic)

your point home.

Number the Stars by Lois Lowry

You are <u>Annemarie</u>. Write a <u>news article</u> for *De Frie Danske* secretly <u>informing</u> <u>the Danish resistance</u>
     (Role)   (Format)   (Strong verb)   (Audience)

of <u>how to obtain a special handkerchief</u>. Try not to give away any secrets to Nazi soldiers who
      (Topic)

might read the article.

Out of the Dust by Karen Hesse

You are <u>Billie Jo</u> and wonder <u>why your family stays in Oklahoma</u> after the death of your mother.
    (Role) and (Audience)   (Topic)

Create <u>two free-verse poems</u> to help you work out these feelings. In the first, <u>explain</u> all the
      (Format)   (Strong verb)

reasons you think you should stay, and in the second, <u>share</u> all the reasons you think you should
                                             (Strong verb)

go away from this harsh place.

The Midwife's Apprentice by Karen Cushman

You are <u>Beetle</u> and are tired of being teased as you walk through the village. Write a <u>diary entry</u>
    (Role) and (Audience)   (Format)

<u>outlining</u> <u>how you might escape being constantly teased by the village boys</u>. Be sure to mention the
(Strong verb)   (Topic)

times and places when you think you'll need a good plan.

The Watsons Go to Birmingham—1963 by Christopher Paul Curtis

You are <u>Kenny</u>. At dinner, you want to tell <u>the family</u> <u>your version of what happened that morning</u>
    (Role)   (Audience)   (Topic)

at the church. Write the <u>story</u> you plan to <u>relate</u>, being sure to include your personal observations
                     (Format)   (Strong verb)

and insights about the bombing and how it will affect your family and community.

Writing to Prompts in the Trait-Based Classroom: Literature Response   Scholastic Teaching Resources

The Whipping Boy by Sid Fleischman

When Hold-Your-Nose Billy and Cutwater think you and the prince have changed places, a

plan pops into your head. As <u>Jemmy</u>, write the urgent <u>plea</u> you might present to the reluctant
              (Role)   **(Format)**

<u>Prince Brat</u>, to <u>request</u> that he <u>go along with your plan to trick the prince-nappers</u>.
 (Audience)   **(Strong verb)**   **(Topic)**

The Winter Room by Gary Paulsen

You are <u>Eldon</u> and you love all of the sights and sounds on the farm during the year. Write a <u>poem</u>
     (Role)   **(Format)**

for <u>Mrs. Halverson</u> <u>describing</u> <u>your favorite season on the farm</u>. With your poem, paint a picture of
   (Audience)   **(Strong verb)**   **(Topic)**

that season using as many sensory words as you can.

FANTASY FICTION

Afternoon of the Elves by Janet Taylor Lisle

Your friends are concerned about your new friendship with Sara-Kate. As <u>Hillary</u>, write a <u>note</u>
                                              (Role)   **(Format)**

you might pass to <u>Alison and Jane</u> at school to <u>convince</u> them that <u>there is a real elf village in</u>
         (Audience)   **(Strong verb)**   **(Topic)**

<u>Sara-Kate's backyard</u>. Include several of the details about the village that made you believe it was real.

Gathering Blue by Lois Lowry

You are <u>Matt</u> and you're getting ready to guide Kira's father back home. Write a <u>set of directions</u>
     (Role)   **(Format)**

for <u>Kira</u> that <u>reconstructs</u> <u>your journey to the village of the healing</u>, so she may follow it if she
(Audience)   **(Strong verb)**   **(Topic)**

wishes to see her father. Include some important landmarks to serve as guideposts along the way.

Harry Potter and the Sorcerer's Stone by J. K. Rowling

You are the giant, <u>Hagrid</u>, from Hogwarts. In a <u>conversation</u> with <u>Professor Dumbledore</u>, <u>reflect</u> on
               (Role)   **(Format)**   **(Audience)**   **(Strong verb)**

<u>several different things you will do to keep Harry Potter safe</u> once he arrives at school and begins
           (Topic)

his classes. Since Lord Voldemort will not stay silent once he learns that Harry has come of age, be

sure to include ways that Harry can protect himself from the Dark Lord, too.

Writing to Promote in the Trait-Based Classroom: Literature Response Scholastic Teaching Resources

James and the Giant Peach by Roald Dahl

You are <u>James</u> and you know it is time to leave your aunts' house. Write a <u>good-bye note</u> to
      (Role)   **(Format)**
<u>Aunt Sponge and Aunt Spiker</u> before you climb into the giant peach. In your note, <u>defend</u>
    (Audience)   **(Strong verb)**
<u>your reasons for leaving</u> so that they will really understand.
     (Topic)

Matilda by Roald Dahl

You are <u>Matilda</u> and you are interested in everything about your new psychic gift. Write a
      (Role) and (Audience)
<u>diary entry</u> <u>examining</u> <u>how you feel before, during, and after you move things with your mind</u>.
  (Format)   **(Strong verb)**   **(Topic)**
Use lots of details to describe your sensory experiences.

Midnight Magic by Avi

You are <u>Count Scarazoni</u> and you realize that this ghost may stop you from attaining your goals.
      (Role)
Write an <u>announcement</u> to give before <u>Princess Teresina</u> <u>informing</u> her of <u>your intentions to marry</u>
       (Format)   **(Audience)**   **(Strong verb)**   **(Topic)**
<u>her, ghost or no ghost</u>. Include at least three reasons for her to believe it will happen.

The Book of Three by Lloyd Alexander

You are <u>Prince Gwydion</u> and you have summoned all of your companions to the Great Hall of Caer
      (Role)
Dathyl. Write a <u>royal proclamation</u> to deliver to <u>Fflewddur Fflam, Doli, Gurgi, Eilonwy, and Taran,</u>
          (Format)   **(Audience)**
<u>announcing</u> the <u>gifts you will bestow upon each of them for their bravery</u>.
(Strong verb)   **(Topic)**

The Indian in the Cupboard by Lynne Reid Banks

You are an <u>Iroquois elder</u> and Little Bear has asked you to explain to <u>Omri</u> how a tiny Indian can
     (Role)   **(Audience)**
mysteriously appear. Create an <u>old Indian legend</u> to <u>reveal</u> <u>how the Indian wound up in the cupboard</u>.
                          (Format)   **(Strong verb)**   **(Topic)**

The Little Prince by Antoine de Saint-Exupéry

You are <u>the Little Prince</u> and you have visited seven planets and talked with several
      (Role)
adults. Write the <u>travelogue entries</u> that you might have kept for the <u>pilot</u>, <u>describing</u>
          (Format)   **(Audience) (Strong verb)**
<u>the strangeness of the adults on the planets you visit</u>.
       (Topic)

The Moorchild by Eloise McGraw

You are <u>Saaski</u>. Write a <u>poem</u> to <u>Anwara and Yanno</u> <u>describing</u> the <u>times you felt that</u>
     (Role)   (Format)   (Audience)   (Strong verb)   (Topic)
<u>strange feeling of love</u> while growing up in their household. In your poem, include at least two

situations when you felt their love for you and two situations when you felt love for them.

The Phantom Tollbooth by Norton Juster

Tock hates to waste time. In fact, if he wastes time, an alarm goes off on the clock in his stomach.

As <u>Tock</u>, write a <u>daily schedule</u> to share with <u>Milo</u> <u>describing</u> <u>a typical day in Dictionopolis, where</u>
   (Role)   (Format)   (Audience) (Strong verb)   (Topic)
<u>no time is wasted and no alarm sounds</u>.

The Spiderwick Chronicles, Book 1: The Field Guide by Holly Black and Tony DiTerlizzi

You are <u>Jared</u> and you have discovered the secret room in the attic once occupied by an old relative, Arthur
     (Role)
Spiderwick. Create a <u>map</u> of the house with directions for <u>exploring</u> <u>the secret room of Arthur Spiderwick,</u>
               (Format)   (Strong verb)   (Topic)
so <u>Simon and Mallory</u> can join you as you investigate all the secrets of this mysterious place.
    (Audience)

Tuck Everlasting by Natalie Babbitt

The <u>Disney Studio executives</u> are looking for a theme song for the new movie version of *Tuck*
     (Audience)
Everlasting. As <u>Winnie</u>, compose the <u>lyrics for a song</u> that <u>extol</u> <u>the miracle of everlasting life</u>.
     (Role)   (Format)   (Strong verb)   (Topic)

Walk Two Moons by Sharon Creech

You are <u>Chanhassen</u>, who has left home without explanation. Write a series of <u>post cards with</u>
     (Role)   (Format)
<u>illustrations</u> from all the places you go to send to <u>Salamanca and her father</u> so they have a few
                                      (Audience)
clues to <u>determine</u> <u>where you have gone</u>. Include the reasons why you stopped at each place to
   (Strong verb)   (Topic)
provide your family with information to help them understand your actions.

Writing to Prompts in the Trait-Based Classroom: Literature Response · Scholastic Teaching Resources

Creating Your Own R.A.F.T.S. Prompts

Once you and your students are comfortable using the ready-to-use R.A.F.T.S., you may wish to create your own based on books that have become classroom favorites. Imagine that your class has just finished reading the book *Frindle* by Andrew Clements. Using the blank reproducible grid on page 77, choose the R.A.F.T.S. components that you want to use. You might take characters and situations directly from the book, or stretch students' imaginations by using components suggested by ideas or story lines in the book. For example:

Role:	advertising executive
Audience:	advertising team
Format:	announcement
Topic:	new ad campaign for Frindles
Strong Verb:	motivate

Once you have completed a grid, take the five components and create a paragraph. Underline and label each component so that it is clear to students.

You are a big-shot <u>advertising executive</u> for the Frindle Company.
(Role)
Write an <u>announcement</u> to <u>motivate</u> your <u>advertising team</u> with news
(Format) **(Strong verb)** **(Audience)**
of a <u>new ad campaign for Frindles</u>.
(Topic)

Then, write your R.A.F.T.S. paragraph on the board or make photocopies—and have students start writing. You can help students work on the traits of writing by pointing out the traits that support each component, as shown below:

Role:	advertising executive (voice and word choice)
Audience:	advertising team (voice and word choice)
Format:	announcement (organization)
Topic:	new ad campaign for Frindles (ideas)
Strong Verb:	motivate (ideas, organization, voice, word choice, sentence fluency, and conventions)

With this defined **R**ole, your students will find themselves writing not as themselves—but as advertising executives. In this role, they can express themselves in a new **voice** and with interesting **word choices**. Since they're writing for a specific **A**udience, an advertising team, they must also communicate their message using appropriate **voice** and **word choices**. Because they're given a defined **F**ormat, an announcement, your students must also focus their attention on the **organization** of the writing. (See page 78 for an extensive list of possible formats.) The **T**opic is inspired by **ideas** from the book. And lastly, with a **S**trong verb, they must motivate their audience with interesting **ideas** effective **organization**, appropriate **voice**, interesting **word choice**, smooth **sentence fluency**, and correct **conventions**. (See page 79 for an extensive list of possible strong verbs.)

A sixth grader's writing based on the *Frindle* R.A.F.T.S. prompt

Ladies and Gentlemen:

Today we are meeting to unveil my new advertising plan for Frindles—the wonder writing tool of the twenty-first century.

As you know, our company stock has skyrocketed since we acquired the Frindle line. People just can't buy them fast enough. Our factories and distribution centers are working around the clock to fill orders from all over the world.

I am pleased to announce that as of today we will be marketing via TV, newspapers, and magazines, and we have taken out ad space on Internet search engines, too. We have the exclusive rights to market and advertise for Frindle so expect to be very busy in the next few months.

You will need to work extra hard on the advertising campaign in the next few days. Cancel your vacations, plan to sleep here at the office. Frindles is going to keep you so busy there won't be time for anything else. Clean out your desks of other, obsolete writing implements. From now on, this is a Frindles-only workplace.

After introducing the basic R.A.F.T.S. format, just think of how students will be concentrating on the traits in all writing assignments. R.A.F.T.S. prompts and writing traits go hand-in-hand to help your students focus their writing for success!

BOOK TITLE: _____

ROLE: _____

AUDIENCE: _____

FORMAT: _____

TOPIC: _____

STRONG VERB: _____

BOOK TITLE: _____

ROLE: _____

AUDIENCE: _____

FORMAT: _____

TOPIC: _____

STRONG VERB: _____

BOOK TITLE: _____

ROLE: _____

AUDIENCE: _____

FORMAT: _____

TOPIC: _____

STRONG VERB: _____

FORMATS TO CONSIDER
WHEN CREATING YOUR OWN PROMPTS

advertisement

anecdote

announcement

application

biographical sketch

blurb

board game

brochure

caption

commentary

consumer guide

contest entry

critique

Dear Abby letter

debate

definition

dialogue

diary entry

dictionary entry

directions

discussion

editorial

e-mail

encyclopedia entry

epitaph

eulogy

free verse poem

graffiti

greeting card

historical account

instructions

interview

introduction

journal entry

last will and testament

lecture

legislation

lesson plan

letter

letter to the editor

list

map

math problem

memo

menu

monologue

motto

newspaper article

note

oration

package copy

parody

personalized license plate

poems

post card

poster

prediction

prophecy

puzzle

rebuttal

request

résumé

review

screen play

sermon

ship log

short story

skit

slogan

song

speech

stream of consciousness

summary

survival manual

telegram

telephone dialogue

test questions

thumbnail sketch

top-ten list

travelogue

wanted poster

word puzzle

STRONG VERBS TO CONSIDER
WHEN CREATING YOUR OWN PROMPTS

advise	defend	participate
align	define	persuade
amaze	describe	predict
analyze	determine	quote
announce	diagnose	realize
annoy	divulge	reconcile
appeal	embellish	reconstruct
apply	empathize	record
assimilate	encourage	reflect
brainstorm	engrave	reject
browse	enlighten	relate
capture	examine	remember
carve	exemplify	remind
censor	explain	request
characterize	explore	reveal
charge	express	review
clarify	extol	script
coalesce	highlight	scrutinize
combine	hoodwink	search
communicate	identify	shape
compare	illuminate	showcase
connect	imagine	specify
connive	improvise	summarize
consider	inform	suppress
construct	inspect	trigger
contemplate	introduce	urge
convince	investigate	visualize
create	mold	warn
critique	motivate	write
decipher	outline	

Bibliography

Across Five Aprils by Irene Hunt (Berkley Publishing Group, 1999).

Afternoon of the Elves by Janet Taylor Lisle (Orchard Books, 1989).

A Year Down Yonder by Richard Peck (Dial Books For Young Readers, 2000).

The Book of Three by Lloyd Alexander (Holt, Rinehart, and Wintson, 1964).

Bridge to Terabithia by Katherine Paterson (HarperCollins, 1977).

Bud, Not Buddy by Christopher Paul Curtis (Delacorte Press, 1999).

Crispin: The Cross of Lead by Avi (Hyperion Books for Children, 2002).

Dear Mr. Henshaw by Beverly Cleary (William Morrow & Company, Inc., 1983).

Everything on a Waffle by Polly Horvath (Farrar, Straus and Giroux, 2001).

Fig Pudding by Ralph Fletcher (Clarion Books, 1995).

Frindle by Andrew Clements (Simon & Schuster Books for Young Readers, 1996).

From the Mixed-up Files of Mrs. Basil E. Frankweiler by E. L. Konigsburg (Atheneum Books for Young Readers, 1967).

Gathering Blue by Lois Lowry (Houghton Mifflin, 2000).

Harris and Me: A Summer Remembered by Gary Paulsen (Harcourt Brace & Company, 1993).

Harry Potter and the Sorcerer's Stone by J. K. Rowling (Scholastic Press, 1997).

Hatchet by Gary Paulsen (Simon & Schuster, 1987).

Holes by Louis Sachar (Farrar, Straus and Giroux, 1998).

Homeless Bird by Gloria Whelan (HarperCollins Publishers, 2000).

Homesick: My Own Story by Jean Fritz (Cornerstone Books, 1987).

Hoot by Carl Hiaasen (Alfred A. Knopf, 2002).

How to Eat Fried Worms by Thomas Rockwell (Franklin Watts, 1973).

The Indian in the Cupboard by Lynne Reid Banks (Doubleday, 1981).

James and the Giant Peach by Roald Dahl (Random House, 1986).

The Little Prince by Antoine de Saint-Exupéry (Harcourt Brace, 1943).

Maniac Magee by Jerry Spinelli (Little, Brown & Company, 1990).

Matilda by Roald Dahl (Viking Kestrel, 1988).

Mick Harte Was Here by Barbara Park (Alfred A. Knopf, 1995).

Midnight Magic by Avi (Scholastic Press, 1999).

The Midwife's Apprentice by Karen Cushman (Clarion Books, 1995).

The Moorchild by Eloise McGraw (Margaret K. McElderry Books, 1996).

Number the Stars by Lois Lowry (Houghton Mifflin, 1989).

Out of the Dust by Karen Hesse (Scholastic Press, 1997).

Tales of a Fourth Grade Nothing by Judy Blume (E. P. Dutton, 1972).

Tangerine by Edward Bloor (Harcourt Brace & Company, 1997).

The Outsiders by S. E. Hinton (Viking Press, 1967).

The Phantom Tollbooth by Norton Juster (Random House, 1961).

The Spiderwick Chronicles, Book 1: The Field Guide by Holly Black and Tony DiTerlizzi (Simon and Schuster, 2003).

The View from Saturday by E. L. Konigsburg (Atheneum Books for Young Readers, 1996).

Tuck Everlasting by Natalie Babbitt (Farrar, Straus and Giroux, 1975).

Walk Two Moons by Sharon Creech (HarperCollins Publishers, 1994).

The Watsons Go to Birmingham—1963 by Christopher Paul Curtis (Delacorte Press, 1995).

What Jamie Saw by Carolyn Coman (Front Street, Inc., 1995).

Where the Red Fern Grows: The Story of Two Dogs and a Boy by Wilson Rawls (Doubleday, 1961).

The Whipping Boy by Sid Fleischman (William Morrow & Company, New York, 1986).

The Winter Room by Gary Paulsen (Orchard Books, 1989).